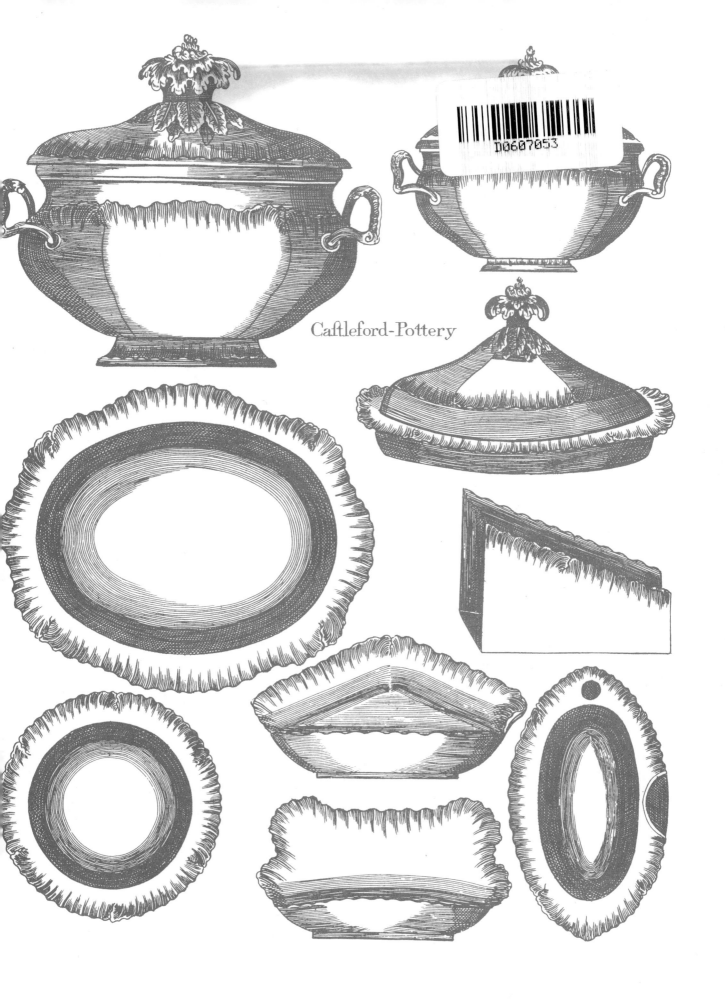

Caftleford-Pottery

Pottery

THE SMITHSONIAN ILLUSTRATED LIBRARY OF ANTIQUES

General Editor: Brenda Gilchrist

Pottery

Compiled for the Cooper-Hewitt Museum

COOPER-HEWITT MUSEUM

The Smithsonian Institution's National Museum of Design

ENDPAPERS
Selection of patterns for assorted pottery from *The Castleford Pottery Pattern Book*, Castleford, England, 1796. Royal Doulton Tableware Ltd.

FRONTISPIECE
Maiolica dish showing *The Rape of Helen of Troy*, after an engraving attributed to Marcantonio Raimondi. Italian, Urbino, about 1540–50. Diameter: 47 cm. (18½ in.). Unmarked. Metropolitan Museum of Art, New York, Samuel D. Lee Fund, 1941

Art Direction, Design: Joseph B. Del Valle

Text Editor: Carlotta Kerwin

Picture Editor: Lisa Little

Contents

1 Introduction

Legend has it that the earth was shaped on a potter's wheel by Ptah, ancient Egypt's god of craftsmen. The facts prove that pottery is, indeed, a very ancient art. Shards of earthenware containers made nine thousand years ago have been found at Catal Hüyük in Turkey, and there is reason to believe that the idea of baking clay to make useful, and frequently beautiful, vessels sprang up independently in all parts of the prehistoric world, from China to Mesopotamia to Europe.

As well as being the earliest of the so-called minor arts, pottery is perhaps also the most personal. Very few of us can weave an Oriental rug or even create a silver ewer. But everyone can make a pot. All that is needed is malleable clay, hands to shape it and a source of heat to harden the product. The result will be a tangible expression of an individual's need and sense of beauty. As the distinguished British artist-potter Bernard Leach put it: "It seems reasonable to expect that beauty will emerge from a fusion of the individual character and culture of the potter with the nature of his materials—clay, pigment, glaze—and his management of the fire, and that consequently we may hope to find in good pots those innate qualities which we most admire in people."

To appreciate fully how this art of potting evolved from basic sun-baked jugs and urns, made to store food and drink, to the ceramic masterpieces produced, for example, during the T'ang dynasty in medieval China or in eighteenth-century Staffordshire in England, it is helpful to be familiar with the materials and techniques that are fundamental to the art form.

Clay, the sole basic ingredient of pottery, is found in deposits all over the world, although its composition and fineness vary widely. Essentially it is an earthy material made up of tiny mineral particles, frequently mixed with pebbles and other matter. When these are

Colorplate 1.
Grayish-blue glazed earthenware pitcher with nickel lid and rim. The handle is the half-length figure of a satyr. English, Hanley, c. 1834–54. Height: 28.8 cm. (11¼ in.). Mark: octagonal seal containing anchor, vase and label inscribed *W. Ridgway & Co.* Cooper-Hewitt Museum, gift of Sarah Cooper Hewitt

removed and the clay is mixed with water, it becomes a highly plastic substance that can be molded into virtually any desired form.

In the beginning all pottery was shaped by hand. Some early potters simply took lumps of wet clay and by scooping and pressing formed them into vessels. Another method was to knead clay into strips and coil them, one on top of another, until a pot was formed. This coiling was usually done on a board or mat that the potter turned as he manipulated the strips; he then fused them together and smoothed them with his fingers.

The turning and shaping process was made far easier by the potter's wheel, which was invented in remote times and in several parts of the world. The potter places a mass of wet clay in the center of a horizontal wheel that rotates easily on an axle. The potter's hands, pressing on the constantly revolving clay, shape the pot, which naturally assumes an overall circular form. When the clay, guided by the craftsman's fingers, has become a pot of the desired height and shape, it is cut from the wheel and set aside to dry. This technique has traditionally been known as *throwing* a pot; it is still used today by potters who produce wares by hand.

Pottery is also made by pouring liquid clay into molds made of baked clay or, in modern times, of plaster of paris. *Molding*, although quite ancient, made possible the commercial mass production of pottery, since many pieces could be produced from a single mold.

Once a pot is formed, it must be dried and exposed to heat—or *fired*—above a temperature of about 500 degrees Celsius. At this heat physical changes occur within the clay, with the result that it hardens permanently and retains the desired shape. When certain types of clay are fired above 1200 degrees Celsius, additional changes take place and the clay *vitrifies*—that is, becomes as hard and as impervious to liquids as glass. All clays can be fired to the temperature needed to ensure hardness, but not all can tolerate the intense heat needed for vitrification. The most common clays—such as red clay, which is familiar all over the world—are composed of very fine particles and cannot be fired above about 1150 degrees Celsius without melting. Pottery fired at these lower temperatures is known as *earthenware*. Although hard and brittle, it is slightly porous and requires further surface treatment if it is to be impervious to liquid. Coarser clays, on the other hand, have a higher fluxing temperature, and wares made from such clays can be fired to the vitrification level to become non-porous. Such hard-baked pottery is commonly called *stoneware*.

In many primitive cultures, simple earthenware was, and still is, baked by the sun. But some peoples discovered very early that pots could be hardened more effectively in a fire. From that discovery came the idea of firing a pot in an oven, called a *kiln*, which is still the method in general use. Today's kilns are sophisticated affairs, capable of attaining high and precisely regulated temperatures. The temperature

Figure 1.
A potter's workshop. Line engraving after a
painting by Édouard Dantan. French, late
nineteenth century. Cooper-Hewitt Museum
Picture Library

and the atmosphere in the kiln—the level of oxygen and carbon
monoxide—combine with the chemical composition of the clay to
produce the color of the baked pot. Fine earthenware clay, which
generally contains a high level of iron particles, fires to shades ranging
from buff to dark red unless the amount of oxygen in the kiln is re-
duced. In that case it becomes gray or even black. Stoneware clays,
containing less iron, usually fire to the more neutral grays and blacks.

The oldest methods of decorating a pot, again still in use today, are
incising and making designs with *slip*, a mixture of fine clay and
water. Incised motifs are simply cut into the unbaked clay with a
sharp instrument, a knife or even a pointed stick. Slip, which is
usually creamy in both consistency and color, can be *trailed*—that
is, dripped from a spout—onto the dry but unbaked surface of a pot
in various patterns; or an entire pot can be dipped into it. Then a

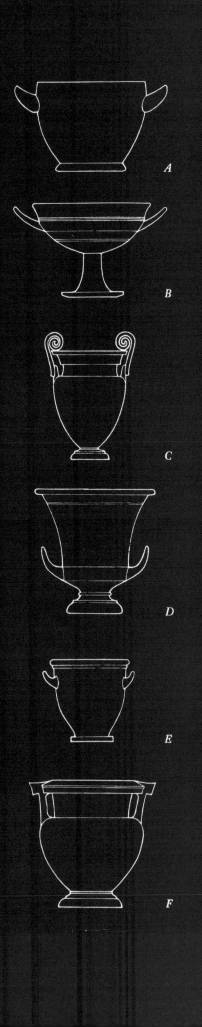

design scratched through a coating of slip will reveal the clay beneath, normally of a different color. A term of Italian origin, *sgraffito*, has been applied to this technique.

Also very ancient is the practice of glazing the surface of a pot for both decorative and practical reasons. A *glaze*, as the name implies, is a coating—usually applied in liquid form—that becomes glassy when applied to hardened clay and fired. A surprising variety of substances interact with clay when heated in a kiln to produce such a vitreous sheath: lead oxide, tin oxide and soda, to name just three. Many of these glazing agents also produce colors when fired, and a very wide variety of shades can be obtained by altering the atmosphere inside the kiln during firing. Thus glazes serve to decorate earthenware pottery as well as to give it a hard surface impervious to liquids. Lead glaze is one of the easiest to use, and historically it has been one of the most important. The introduction of tin glaze to Europe led to a famous and beautiful class of European ceramics: tin-glaze pottery includes Italian maiolica, French faience and Dutch and English delftware.

Plain salt, simply thrown into the kiln by the shovelful during firing, may be used to produce glazes for stoneware. The soda in the salt, volatilized by heat, combines with the silica and alumina normally present in stoneware clay to form a glaze that is both hard and attractively irregular in texture. Salt-glazed stoneware plays a major role in German, English and American ceramic history.

Although glazes provide color, such overall decoration has not satisfied potters through the ages. Much of the finest pottery has been further embellished with metallic oxides, from which many colors can be made; for example, cobalt produces shades of blue, manganese makes tones of red, brown and purple, and antimony creates yellow. Color may be painted onto the pot with a brush in one of two ways. In the method called *underglaze painting*, the painted design is applied to a pot that has been fired to hardness but not yet glazed. The pottery is then glazed and fired again. Not many colors can withstand the high temperature required to fix a glaze, so underglaze painting has been limited to colors that react best to heat. Blue and red are the most commonly used. A greater range of colors can be employed if the painting is applied after the pot has been glazed, in the technique of *overglaze painting*. These *enamel colors* are then fixed to the glaze by a second firing, at a relatively low temperature. Glazed and painted pottery can be made even richer by the application of a metallic sheen, produced by adding powdered copper, silver or platinum to an additional glaze. Known as *luster*, this technique had its origins in the Near East and is particularly important in Islamic and Spanish pottery.

Although people today, as in times past, do collect the work of living potters, most collectors have turned their attention to older

Figure 2.
Greek vases. *A*. Skyphos. *B*. Kylix. *C*. Volute krater. *D*. Calyx krater. *E*. Bell krater. *F*. Column krater. *G*. Oenochoe. *H*. Oenochoe (chous). *I*. Lekythos. *J*. Stamnos. *K*. Neck amphora. Oxford University Press

G

H

I

J

K

wares—antique pottery. Since some pottery has been decorated with scenes drawn from the cultures that produced it, antique pottery often provides a window on history, showing the customs and costumes, favorite myths and ideals of beauty that delighted our ancestors. Even abstract patterns can have symbolic meaning and reveal a great deal about religious beliefs. Such motifs frequently offer valuable clues to place of origin as well as to intercultural links.

Pottery has also attracted collectors because of its fascinating variety. For some people the most important criterion lies in the refinement of the craft—the making of wares that are lighter, more delicate, more lustrous and colorful and yet tougher and more resistant. For others, roughness and interesting textures provide greater appeal. Each sort of pottery has its enthusiasts, and although certain narrow areas have become difficult to collect because so few examples remain on the market, many fine wares continue to be in good supply. Indeed, several periods of potting, and the work of certain notable potteries, have been unduly neglected; some of these promising areas will be mentioned in this book. In any case, the collecting of pottery flourishes and all signs indicate that it will continue to do so.

The marks on pottery are an involved subject. They have a long history, going back in the form of signatures and inscriptions to the classical world. Nevertheless, over the ages a great deal of fine pottery has been made and sold without any marks at all. Leading factories in modern times have not always marked their wares, and when they have, the marks have often been inconsistent. Forged marks are common. Although marks are an interesting study and can be a useful guide in collecting, experienced collectors and most authorities on ceramics agree that in determining the quality of a piece, its appearance and feel are more important than any marks it may carry.

Because pottery has diverse origins in many parts of the world, with little historical connection, the story of its development does not lend itself to straight chronological sequence. In this book, the pottery of the classical world, the Near East, the Far East, various European nations and America has been dealt with separately in a roughly chronological way. In each area, the significant types of pottery are discussed, and many of the main producers named.

Beyond the scope of this survey is the pottery that has been created by peoples living in areas far removed from outside cultural influences, notably wares produced in pre-Columbian America, sub-Saharan Africa and Oceania. Some of this work dates back at least to the second millennium B.C. and is particularly admired and emulated by artists of the twentieth century for its remarkable sophistication of form and design. These pottery traditions represent a specialized field, deserving a volume in their own right.

2 Greek, Etruscan and Roman Pottery

Greek Few objects in the world have been more highly regarded through the ages than fine examples of ancient Greek pottery. With extraordinary skill, Greek artists demonstrated the importance of combining functional form with aesthetically appealing shape and decoration, and their wares have been copied, modified and adapted by successive Western cultures for the past two thousand years. Even our word for ceramics comes from the Greek term *keramos*.

Greek pottery has been diligently collected and studied, and important museums usually have permanent collections. The most significant forms of this pottery have been lumped under the category of Greek vases, the word *vase* being used in the old sense of hollow vessel. These vases actually come in several shapes and sizes, reflecting the various purposes for which they were made. The most common forms include the kylix, a shallow drinking cup; the kantharos, a deep cup; the oenochoe, a wine pitcher; the lekythos, a tall olive-oil container; the amphora, a two-handled, narrow-necked storage jar; and (most famous of all) the krater, a flare-rimmed bowl, often large, for mixing wine and water (see figure 2).

These varied forms of Greek vases are highly valued for the skilled pottery making they exhibit—the vessel walls are thin and the shapes elegant. But it is the painted figures, both human and animal, embellishing the necks or the entire bodies of the vessels, that astonish us by their innate loveliness and vigor, and by the matchless portrait of ancient Greek life and culture that they provide. The decorations are all the more remarkable since they were done for the most part in only two colors: the reddish tones of the pottery itself, and a black paint, called *engobe*, that was made from a fine clay mix and rendered especially rich and glossy by careful firing techniques.

Colorplate 2.
A lekythos painted in the red-figure technique, showing the running figure of Hermes. The work is attributed to the Tithonos Painter. Greek, Athenia, from Gela, 480–470 B.C. Height: 35.3 cm. (13¾ in.). Metropolitan Museum of Art, New York, Fletcher Fund, 1925

1

The earliest important styles of vase painting developed in the second millennium B.C., and are known as Minoan in Crete and Mycenaean on the mainland. Minoan wares in particular reflect an exuberant love of idyllic surroundings; their motifs are primarily free, naturalistic renderings of floral and marine life, in the form of flowers, fish and seaweed. But as the millennium drew to a close, the pottery reflected the presence of hostile invaders from the north, and the great era of Minoan art diminished. Mycenaean wares were decorated almost exclusively with stark patterns of straight and curvilinear lines. Kraters were a form typical of this early style, which has been aptly termed *geometric*.

Around the middle of the eighth century B.C., vase painters in Attica, the part of ancient Greece that included Athens, began decorating vases with black-stick figures of men and animals. But so stylized were the figures, with triangular torsos and matchstick limbs, that they are still considered geometric. About a century later the vase painters of Corinth, the other main Greek vase-making center, developed the so-called *black figure* technique, a major new development. More realistic figures of people and animals were drawn in black silhouette on the reddish clay ground, and details incised in the black-painted areas before firing. Two other colors, white and purple, were sometimes added to enhance flesh tones or costume detail. The Attic vase painters eventually adopted Corinthian techniques (plate 1), and by 630 B.C. were producing robust, vivid scenes of religious ceremonies, athletic events and above all the lives of mythological gods and goddesses, heroes and heroines.

In the later sixth century B.C. both Attic and Corinthian vase painters made another breakthrough, reversing their color scheme so that the figures were now in the red of the clay base and the backgrounds black. In this *red-figure* technique, the black was laid on around the figures, which were left unpainted or *reserved*. The red figures leap dramatically from the lustrous black surrounding them (colorplate 2). Details within the red reserves were added with black paint, which enabled the painters to limn the folds of drapery, facial expressions and other subtleties they could not achieve before.

The names of a few Greek vase painters have survived—we know of Makron, Exekias, Douris and Euphronios, among others—since they signed their works; but most of the great decorated vases are anonymous and will always be so. Because of stylistic similarities, we do sometimes know the workship where a vase originated, if not the name of the artist who made it. In other cases we know that several vases must have been done by the same person (see plate 1), even if we do not know his name.

The majority of Greek pottery—that intended for daily use—was of course not elaborately decorated, if at all. Most of it is graceful in form; some of the plain black glazed Greek ware is very handsome indeed and remains much sought after.

1.
Greek drinking cup (kylix) decorated in the black-figure style by an anonymous artist who has been given the name of Heidelberg Painter by art historians. The scene depicts two groups of men armed with spears flanking a central figure holding a drinking horn. Greek, Attic, mid-sixth century B.C. Diameter: 62 cm. (24⅛ in.). Height: 13.5 cm. (5¼ in.). Unmarked. Cooper-Hewitt Museum, anonymous gift

2.
Etruscan terra-cotta vase of the two-handled kantharos form decorated in the red-figure style, showing griffins attacking a deer. Fourth century B.C. Height: 15.7 cm. (6¼ in.). Unmarked. Metropolitan Museum of Art, New York, Rogers Fund, 1951

2

Etruscan   The ancient Etruscans dominated parts of the Italian peninsula, principally today's Tuscany, from about 800 B.C. until their final defeat by the emergent Romans about 396 B.C., and certain Greek pottery forms were copied by the Etruscan craftsmen. The Etruscan civilization reached its high point around 500 B.C., when its artisans, especially the metalworkers and potters, attained notable degrees of skill. These craftsmen made wares that show clear Greek influence in their shape and decoration (plate 2). The Greek technique is also evident in the type of Etruscan pottery called *bucchero*, or gray ware, which was fired to a shiny black finish.

This black pottery, in shapes ranging from simple vessels to animal figures or portrait heads, was sometimes painted in white or polychrome. Examples are known from as early as the eighth century B.C., the earlier wares being usually decorated with incised or engraved geometric designs. About two centuries later, bird and animal motifs, highly stylized, were popular. Allover relief patterns were also used later; these were made with carved rollers pressed into the still-soft clay.

Much Etruscan pottery was intended for funerary purposes (plate 3): there were covered burial urns for ashes, and impressive sarcophagi with lifesize figures reclining on the heavy lids. Portrait heads, busts and even some lifesize terra-cotta statues of deities were made during the last fading years of the Etruscan civilization.

Roman   The Roman pottery, which was frequently mass-produced, is not generally distinguished. The best of it is called Arretine, named for Arretium (modern Arezzo, near Florence), where it was first made, probably in a workshop staffed by imported Greek craftsmen. The pottery produced there for a rather brief span—about 30 B.C. to A.D. 30—is also known as red gloss for its bright red glaze, achieved by dipping a completed piece into a mixture of clay and water before firing. Arretine ware was normally formed in molds, which often had designs incised within them. The clay emerged bearing these designs, usually reliefs of classical figures set off by stylized decorative motifs. This molded-relief method, inspired by metalworking techniques, was commonly termed *terra sigillata* ("sealed" or "stamped clay"). The handsome, glossy ware was produced in substantial quantities and widely exported. Its fame became such that it was imitated in many Roman provinces, from Gaul and Britain in the west to North Africa and Asia Minor.

3.
The Etruscans burned their dead and deposited the ashes in cinerary urns that, in the very earliest years of their civilization, were fashioned by hand from volcanic clay. Fluted funerary urn, Etruscan, ninth–seventh century B.C. Height: 46.5 cm. (18¼ in.). Unmarked. Cooper-Hewitt Museum, gift of Karen Johnson Keland

3 The Far Eastern Potters

Pottery making in the Far East dates back at least to Neolithic times. Earthenware pots created for basic household needs more than four thousand years before Christ have been unearthed at the sites of ancient village settlements in China and Japan.

China Semilegendary records tell of the appointment of a "superintendent of pottery" by the so-called Yellow Emperor of China in the third millennium B.C., demonstrating the importance of these craftsmen in antiquity. Their skill—and that of their successors—is revealed by the fact that they used the potter's wheel between the third and second millennia B.C. and were able to control firing at a very early date. High-temperature glazes and stonewares were produced by about 1300 B.C., low-temperature lead glazes by the third century B.C.

There followed a brilliant history of earthenware and stoneware pottery that lasted for about a thousand years until porcelain was developed and supplanted pottery in desirability. During this time China produced an extraordinarily rich variety of ceramic forms and designs, in turn influencing the potter's craft throughout the Far East. This influence was particularly important to Japan and Korea, where Chinese wares inspired craftsmen to create great pottery reflecting their own cultures.

The earliest Chinese pottery existing in sufficient amounts to be collected is that of the Han dynasty (206 B.C.–A.D. 220). Some Han stonewares—typically in the form of funerary urns covered with a soft yellowish, greenish and brownish glaze—were modeled after the great bronzes of earlier periods, but naturalistic motifs began to be introduced in this era. For funerary purposes, many lead-glazed earthenware miniature figurines and replicas of objects from daily life were created.

Colorplate 3.
T'ang dynasty, first half of the eighth century the dead in their tombs are among the best-known Chinese ceramics in the Western world, where they have been long valued for their realistic and human qualities. This aristocratic T'ang lady sits astride a horse. Earthenware with three-color glaze. Chinese, T'ang dynasty, first half of the eighth century. Height: 37.6 cm. (14⅞ in.). Unmarked. Freer Gallery of Art

4.
Covered box of Yüeh ware, an ancient type
of Chinese pottery taking its name from the
region around Hangchow, shown here in an
example made during the Sung dynasty.
Green-glazed stoneware. Chinese, second
half of the tenth century. Diameter: 13.7 cm.
(5⅜ in.). Unmarked. Freer Gallery of Art

Colorplate 4.
The body of this earthenware vase is buff-
colored; the glazes are amber, green and
yellow and in part transparent. Chinese,
T'ang dynasty, first half of the eighth century. Height: 25.17 cm. (10 in.). Marks:
three elongated spur marks on base. Freer
Gallery of Art

Particularly significant in Chinese ceramic history was the emer-
gence at about this time of a green-glazed stoneware pottery known
as Yüeh ware. The name, believed to have been derived from the site
where it was originally produced, reappears frequently in later centuries (plate 4) as the characteristically Chinese tradition of subtly
green-glazed pottery known as *celadon*, or "secret color," developed.

The wares of the next great period, the brilliant and sophisticated
T'ang dynasty (A.D. 618–906), are of special interest to collectors and
command very high prices on the international art market. T'ang
earthenware was glazed with lead in various colors, but because potters
of this period used a lighter-colored paste than their Han predecessors,
the colors are more vivid and true. Typical of T'ang ware also are the
so-called three-color glazes, generally in shades of yellow, green and
blue, which are allowed to run freely into each other in an effect
similar to that of an abstract watercolor (colorplate 4).

The famous T'ang figurines of men, women and animals are familiar
to most museum-goers. These funerary figures were excavated in
large numbers in the late nineteenth and early twentieth centuries as
the result of the building of railroads in China. The earthenware figures

5

6

5.
Tz'ü-chou-type three-handled ewer with turquoise ground color decorated in black, with a scene showing a sage and a small boy carrying a lute; the other side shows a seated lute player and a listener. The inside is glazed in aubergine color. Chinese, Ming dynasty (1368–1644). Height: 21.3 cm. (8⅜ in.). Unmarked. Metropolitan Museum of Art, New York, gift of Robert E. Tod, 1938

6.
Incense burner of light buff-colored clay with green glaze and molded decoration of studs, medallions and scrolls. Chinese, Ming dynasty (1368–1644). Height: 35 cm. 13¾ in.). Unmarked. Metropolitan Museum of Art, New York, bequest of Mrs. H. O. Havemeyer, 1929, H. O. Havemeyer Collection

were made from molds, and were generally lead-glazed in a wide variety of colors, of which green (from copper) and amber and brown (from iron) were the most common; sometimes the faces and hands were painted with pigments after firing. Courtiers, warriors, acrobats, officials and musicians are shown in many poses, standing and sitting, singing and dancing, or riding horses (see colorplate 3); some are only inches high, others several feet tall. These figures are greatly admired for their realism and astonishing vitality, and their appearance and attitudes reveal daily life in China in a way that has timeless fascination.

The last great period of Chinese pottery was that of the Sung dynasty (A.D. 960–1279), when porcelain, which had been developed in the T'ang period, began to supersede pottery in appeal. In this transition period some of the stonewares are referred to as porcellaneous because their qualities verge on those of true porcelain. Most connoisseurs consider the famous Jujao, or Ju, ware to be the finest Sung contribution, and one of the highest achievements of the potter's art. Fewer than forty pieces are known to exist in the West today, mostly in museum collections. Rare even when created in the early twelfth century—it was intended for the court of the emperor—Ju ware is known in bowls, dishes and cupstands, and is characterized by an exquisite, slightly crackled glaze once described as "approaching the blue of the sky after rain."

Sung stonewares of many different types generally referred to as Tz'ü-chou ware are named after a region of north China. The body of the pottery was not always the same; sometimes it was white, sometimes gray, sometimes buff-colored. Typical shapes included vases, pillows (headrests), figurines and jars. Various colored glazes were used, and the decoration was extraordinarily diverse. Tz'ü-chou ware was carved, incised, molded, painted with slip and scratched with sgraffito designs. In the technique of sgraffito, the piece was first covered with slip—usually white—then areas were carved away in the decorator's design; when it was glazed and fired, the body showed through, making the sgraffito pattern. Flowers, birds, fish and human figures were among the subjects of these designs.

Another type of pottery from the Sung dynasty is known as Chün ware. Its characteristic blue glaze was derived from iron—fired with little ventilation in order to reduce the amount of oxygen in the kiln—and its splashes of purple were due to locally applied copper. Chün ware (named after the location of the original kilns) consisted mostly of bowls and flowerpots made in specialized shapes, one example being a low-footed bowl used for displaying narcissus. The entire process of producing flowerpots and bowls was so well developed by this time that pieces were catalogued by size and could be ordered by an inventory number.

The production of earthenware and stoneware continued during the Ming (1368–1644) and Ch'ing (1644–1912) dynasties, even though porcelain now absorbed the best efforts of Chinese potters. Many of the articles that had originated in earlier dynasties were still made in large numbers (plate 5), as were such ceremonial wares as incense burners (plate 6). Another important task was to fill the widespread demand for roof tiles, including handsome ornamental figures for the corners (plate 7). Ming pottery, like Ming porcelain, is noted for its floral-inspired decoration (plate 8).

In the late seventeenth and eighteenth centuries a new impetus for the production of pottery resulted from the demand for teapots, which were exported to the European Continent in great numbers. Tea was just establishing itself as a popular beverage there, and the teapot came along with it from China. Yi-hsing teapots, made of red or brown unglazed stoneware, sometimes incised or decorated in low relief, were the most influential form. Other types of stoneware and earthenware were produced throughout the eighteenth and nineteenth centuries in many Chinese provinces, but in comparison with earlier pottery and with porcelain, these pieces have been little studied and collected in the West.

7

7.
In China, pottery tiles for roofing were glazed in many colors and included figures used for decoration, particularly of roof corners and tops. Mounted warrior roof tile, glazed in brown and green. Chinese, Ming dynasty (1368–1644). Height: 28 cm. (11 in.). Unmarked. Metropolitan Museum of Art, New York, Rogers Fund, 1910

8.
Ming pottery is especially known for its elaborate painted decoration. Earthenware vase decorated with colored enamel reliefs on a turquoise ground. Chinese, Ming dynasty, Wan Li period (1573–1619). Height: 39 cm. (15⅜ in.). Unmarked. Metropolitan Museum of Art, New York, Rogers Fund, 1917

Japan   In Japan, sophisticated stoneware was being made by the fifth century A.D., some of it ash-glazed. But the greatest impulse for making fine pottery came with the introduction of tea and the tea ceremony, which was to become a permanent cultural feature of Japanese life. During the Kamakura period, which began in the late twelfth century, a greenish-yellowish glazed pottery called Seto ware—strongly influenced by the Sung pottery of China—started to be produced in the form of tea utensils. But the tea ceremony assumed its fixed and complicated form in the Momoyama period (1573–1614).

One of the most famous wares of this era was the earthenware Raku tea bowl (plate 9). Hand-molded Raku is fired at low temperatures for periods of as many as five to eight days. Ashes from the long firing are mixed with the glaze, usually black, red or white, to produce a mottled effect. According to tradition, a Korean or Chinese emigrant potter named Chojiro produced bowls so exquisite that they won the praise of a great sixteenth-century tea master. Chojiro's son was given a seal for these wares, bearing the ideograph *raku*, meaning pleasure or enjoyment, and a long family dynasty of Raku potters was established.

Other utensils of this period were stoneware. One of the most notable forms, known as Karatsu ware, was introduced when Korean potters were brought back by Japanese feudal lords during forays of the 1590s into Korea. Typical was a light brushwork effect, as well as the use of contrasting dark and light drip glazes (plate 10). Karatsu ware, in varying styles, was produced well into the eighteenth century (plate 11).

The pottery of Japan has been avidly collected in the West ever since the islands were opened to Western visitors in the mid-nineteenth century, when a detailed Occidental study of Japanese pottery began. Today there are important collections in the United States and in Europe. Japan also has a strong tradition of the artist-potter. In the nineteenth and twentieth centuries very distinguished pieces have been made by these craftsmen, whose work has proved the direct inspiration for several noted European artist-potters.

Korea   Korea too has a notable pottery tradition. Beginning in the eighth century, stoneware was used for funerary pieces, and included large graystone vessels of the Silla period (c. 57 B.C.–A.D. 935), similar to those of T'ang but with pierced designs. Korean potters of the twelfth and thirteenth centuries developed fine glazes, especially celadons reflecting Sung influence, and elaborate incised decoration. Known as Korai wares, the works of this period are highly regarded by Western connoisseurs.

9.
Coarse-grained Raku tea bowl attributed to the master potter Honnami Koyetsu (1557–1637), who was also a master calligrapher, painter and lacquer artist. Raku ware is especially esteemed in Japan itself, where fine examples command very high prices. Japanese, Yamashiro Province, about 1600. Diameter: 13.1 cm. (5⅛ in.). Unmarked. Metropolitan Museum of Art, New York, gift of Howard Mansfield, 1936, Howard Mansfield Collection

10.
Stoneware pitcher in the Karatsu style. Japanese, Momoyama period, seventeenth century. Height: 15.8 cm. (6¼ in.). Unmarked. Freer Gallery of Art

11.
Traveler's tea bowl (*cha-wan*) of Karatsu pottery, shown here with accessories including, left to right, a brocade bag for the tea bowl, a cylindrical wooden holder for bamboo whisk and jointed bamboo spoon, a black lacquer tea jar in its bag and a bamboo whisk (in the tea bowl). Japanese, Hizen Province, eighteenth century. Height of tea bowl: 9.6 cm. (3¾ in.). Unmarked. Metropolitan Museum of Art, New York, gift of Howard Mansfield, 1936, Howard Mansfield Collection

10

11

4 Islamic Pottery

We credit the artisans of ancient Greece with developing shapes of vessels that have influenced potters to this day; and to the craftsmen of medieval China we owe the evolution of texture from rude clay to refined porcelain. But it was the Islamic artists of the Near East who perfected the highly decorative, shimmering glazed effects that were to inspire potters for centuries. Fascinated by the interplay of light and shadow, these craftsmen developed an extraordinary variety of colored glazes, of which turquoise—often considered to be a charm against evil spirits—was the most prevalent. Even more important in the history of ceramics was the invention of luster painting, a technique that used metallic oxides to impart a sometimes colorful, sometimes mysterious iridescent sheen. This *lusterware*, developed in the Near East, was the direct antecedent of the Hispano-Moresque wares of medieval Spain and the maiolica wares of the Italian Renaissance.

The great centers of Islamic pottery making were located in what is present-day Afghanistan, Iran, Iraq, Syria, Egypt and Turkey. Their history can best be divided into three distinct periods: early (the ninth to eleventh centuries); medieval (the twelfth to fourteenth centuries); and late (the fifteenth to nineteenth centuries).

Until the eighth century, Near Eastern potters continued to produce unglazed and glazed earthenware in the tradition of their ancient forebears. These included the Neolithic potters of Anatolia, who fired and polished handmade pottery with some skill at least as far back as 6500 B.C.; the Assyrians and Babylonians of the Fertile Crescent region, who used the potter's wheel, produced monochrome and polychrome decorations with geometric and animal motifs, and are believed to have made metal-tinged glazes by about 2000 B.C.; and the ancient Egyptians, who created extraordinarily fine monochrome

Colorplate 5.
Deep earthenware bowl with flaring sides decorated over a cream-white glaze, with a scene showing an elephant and riders in blue, green, red, black and gold, surrounded by inscriptions. Iranian, Rayy, Seljuk period, twelfth–thirteenth century. Diameter: 18.6 cm. (7¼ in.). Unmarked. Freer Gallery of Art

pottery in the fifth millennium B.C. Despite waves of invasions such as those of the Hittites and the Sassanians in centuries to come, the traditional methods were followed. Of somewhat minor aesthetic interest, these ancient ceramics have more appeal to historians than to students and collectors of antiques.

In about A.D. 750, outside influences drastically disrupted the traditional ways and triggered an entirely new era in the history of ceramics. At this time the Islamic Empire stretched throughout the Near East all the way to the borders of China, bringing with it radically new design motifs consisting of highly complex geometric and floral patterns and decorative calligraphy. Meanwhile exquisite examples of Chinese glazed earthenware, stoneware and porcelain of the T'ang dynasty (618–906) were being carried into the Near East overland along the great Silk Route and by boat along the sea route around India. In addition, Chinese technical skills—particularly the secret of making a more refined thin paste—are believed to have been brought into the Near East at this time by Chinese prisoners of war captured by the Islamic rulers, the Abbasids, when China attempted an invasion of their Muslim stronghold.

In attempting to copy the much-admired Chinese porcelains, Near Eastern potters acquired a skill for making glazes that has never been equaled. This skill, combined with their artistic use of Islamic decorative designs, resulted in a distinctive new pottery form.

The Early Period Baghdad and Basra in modern-day Iraq were important centers of ceramic development during the early period. Their fine lead-glazed redware was decorated by the sgraffito technique, and splashed and mottled like some T'ang wares of the time. White tinglazed pottery, also showing Chinese influence, was painted with floral, geometric and calligraphic designs in the angular Kufic script. Luster-painted pottery was made by firing a piece of gray or buff pottery, then covering it with an opaque white tin glaze and firing it again to fix the glaze; this in turn was covered with metallic oxides and fired once more. At first, polychrome lusters were used. Later, beginning probably in the tenth century, most lusterware used brown or yellow monochrome (no doubt because it was more difficult and therefore less economical to fire several different metal oxides).

Advanced forms of lusterware were also being made in Egypt, beginning in the tenth century. This pottery, of the Fatimid period, was lavishly painted with birds, animals and human figures. In Persia and Afghanistan, slip-painted pottery of fine-grained earthenware was the outstanding expression of the potter's art at this time. The Nishapur region of northern Persia gave its name to the most famous pottery of this type—glazed dishes and bowls adorned with palmettes and Kufic inscriptions.

The Medieval Period The Seljuk Turks conquered Persia and the neighboring lands in the mid-eleventh century, ushering in the medieval period. During the succeeding two centuries a number of distinguished wares were produced by this culture. In particular, the fifty years between 1175 and 1225 are considered by many authorities to be the greatest single flowering of ceramics in Near Eastern history.

The various categories of Seljuk pottery, which was produced mainly at Rayy (colorplate 5) and Kashan in north-central Persia, include the famous Persian white wares made in imitation of Chinese Ting porcelain of the Sung dynasty. Sometimes incised with floral designs, sometimes pierced and glazed over in an attempt to duplicate the delicate look of real porcelain, these wares are a high point of Islamic ceramic art. Other techniques used on plates, bowls, vases and on an extraordinary variety of wall tiles include silhouette painting in black and turquoise, underglaze and overglaze painting.

Among the most distinguished of Seljuk wares was Mina'i, which took its name from a special method of overglaze painted decoration. Enamel colors were generally painted over an opaque white glaze and then subjected to a second, low-temperature firing. Many of the decorative plates have extremely lively scenes depicting arresting human and animal figures engaged in all sorts of activities (plate 12).

12.
Mina'i ware was decorated in enamels (the word *mina'i* means enamel) painted over the glaze. Below right is a white bowl showing a man mounted on a donkey accompanied by attendants and surrounded by birds, plants and fish, with inscriptions in Kufic and Persian. Directly below is a detail from the same bowl. Made by Abu Zayd Kashani. Iranian, Seljuk, 1187. Diameter: 21.5 cm. (8½ in.). Unmarked. Metropolitan Museum of Art, New York, Fletcher Fund, 1964

12

Some of the scenes shown on Mina'i pottery are taken from stories that were also illustrated in the celebrated Persian manuscripts of the time.

Less spectacular but well worth mention were the medieval pottery centers of Rakka and Rusafa in Syria, which produced attractive glazed wares decorated with figures, foliage and calligraphy. Far to the north, near the Caspian Sea, beautiful white-glazed pieces with simple incised designs, known as Amol ware, were being made, as was pottery with more complicated sgraffito effects known as Aghkand and Gabri. On Aghkand wares, incised lines were used to prevent different-colored glazes from running into each other; on Gabri, the design itself was created by scratching away portions of the glaze to reveal the body color underneath.

In the thirteenth century Mongol invaders from the east caused the destruction of many of the great Islamic pottery centers of medieval times. Least affected, as far as pottery is concerned, was Kashan, where extremely fine ware—much of it luster—was produced uninterruptedly throughout the thirteenth and fourteenth centuries. The first-rate glazed wall tiles, revealing extraordinary variety, give special distinction to the output of this area of central Persia (plate 13).

13.
Pottery wall tiles were designed for many Near Eastern buildings, especially mosques. These are buff-colored with brown luster on an opaque glaze, and are inscribed with passages from the Koran. Iranian, Kashan (?), thirteenth century (several are dated 1264). Width of each: 20.3 cm. (8 in.). Unmarked. Metropolitan Museum of Art, New York, gift of Horace Havemeyer, 1941, H. O. Havemeyer Collection

Another lone outpost was Egypt, then ruled by the Mamluks, who succeeded in holding the Mongols at bay and welcomed refugee potters from overrun territories. In this sanctuary craftsmen created large bowls and storage jars of underglaze blue and black to which the name Mamluk ware has been given.

The Late Period From the fifteenth to the eighteenth century Persia and much of the rest of the Near East, like Europe at that time, were greatly (almost overwhelmingly) under the influence of the widely diffused Chinese blue-and-white porcelain of the Ming dynasty. Scholars now believe that this blue-and-white style of decoration actually originated in the Near East centuries before—but with black outlines—and returned without those outlines to bring fresh inspiration at this time. In any case, Persian rulers and members of the upper classes collected Chinese imports avidly, and the influence of Ming porcelains on local creations can hardly be exaggerated. Some Persian wares were even decorated with Chinese motifs; indeed, imitation went so far that Chinese and Persian outputs have been confused, despite the difference in materials.

During the rule of the Safavids (1502–1736) this Chinese influence was especially strong and took more than one form. A great pottery center at that time was Kirman, far to the east. There, in addition to blue-and-white—sometimes combined on one piece with red and green Islamic designs—craftsmen produced quantities of glazed pottery imitating the celebrated Chinese green-glazed celadon wares. Plain white

14.
White clay tile or plaque with a colorless glaze, decorated in blue, green and red. The design shows parrots on either side of a fountain in a floral setting. Turkish, Iznik, Ottoman period, early seventeenth century. Dimensions: 26 x 24 cm. (10¼ x 9½ in.). Unmarked. Freer Gallery of Art

wares, often with glazed-over pierced decorations attempting to emulate Sung porcelain, were also produced in large numbers. When European traders, especially the Dutch, had trouble getting porcelain from China, they imported some of this Persian ware. Because its place of origin was unknown, it was called Gombroon ware after the port (now Bender Abbas) on the Persian Gulf where it was loaded into Dutch bottoms for transport to Europe.

Two other important pottery types came from extreme ends of the Islamic Empire in the Near East during this late period. In the homes of villagers in remote Kubachi in the Caucasus were found black and turquoise ceramics reminiscent of early Ming pottery; blue-and-white ware; and polychrome ware, with designs including figures in Persian and European dress. Erroneously called Kubachi wares, these pieces have no verifiable place of origin. As Kubachi was a metal-working center without any pottery tradition, it is assumed that the pottery was at one time traded for arms.

Far to the west, across the Bosporus from Istanbul, Turkish craftsmen of the period produced a particularly fine pottery known as Iznik. Iznik pottery is of white clay, most colorfully decorated with cobalt blue, turquoise, purple, black and red under a clear, uncracked glaze. The potteries of Iznik, which were said to have numbered three hundred around the year 1600, produced tiles (plate 14) for numerous buildings constructed by the Ottoman Turks. They also made large plates and dishes, jugs, vases and drinking vessels with vivid decoration including floral and leaf designs (colorplate 6). Connoisseurs believe that the best Iznik products are those of the third quarter of the sixteenth century. Iznik went into decline during the seventeenth century, but the potteries did not finally close until early in the eighteenth century.

Iznik pottery was very widely exported. So much of it was sent to the island of Rhodes that it was thought to have been manufactured there and until quite recently was often called Rhodian pottery. Another theory was that it was made in Syria, which led to the name Damascus ware. The actual origin was not finally determined until excavations were made at Iznik in this century.

Victorian collectors were particularly fond of the so-called Rhodian ware—so much so that even the large quantities Turkish potteries sent to Europe did not suffice for the demand. As a result, skillful forgeries abound.

The nineteenth century brought a decline in the rich tradition of Near Eastern Islamic pottery. Under the Qajar dynasty (1795–1925) pottery remained on the whole backward-looking in design, and owed much to the Persian tradition of showing such princely activities as riding and hawking (plate 15). Qajar wares have so far been comparatively little studied and collected outside Iran.

Colorplate 6.
Earthenware dish with flattened rim, decorated with a floral design in underglaze blue. Turkish, Iznik, Ottoman period, c. 1500. Diameter: 39.3 cm. (15⅛ in.). Unmarked. Freer Gallery of Art

15.
Large earthenware bowl decorated in underglaze blue and black, with a figure riding on a galloping horse and holding a bird, probably a hawk, in one hand. Iranian, Qajar dynasty, nineteenth century. Diameter: 32.7 cm. (12⅞ in.). Unmarked. Freer Gallery of Art

5 Spanish, Portuguese and Italian Pottery

Spain The story of one of Europe's great ceramic traditions begins in Spain in the centuries following the Arab conquest of A.D. 711. In the wake of invading Moors from North Africa came craftsmen who knew the two most important techniques used by the brilliant Islamic potters of the Near East: the art of making a white tin glaze and the secret of luster painting. These skills, combined with local talent and cultural heritage, were to precipitate a unique new style of pottery known first in Spain as Hispano-Moresque and later in Italy as maiolica.

The term *golden pottery* was applied to Hispano-Moresque ware even in the late Middle Ages, when it was first produced, and indicates clearly the value that has always been attached to the work by connoisseurs and collectors alike. This distinctive style is a tin-glazed pottery that has been lustered, or coated with a thin, iridescent metallic film in a process requiring three firings. After a piece was thrown, or pressed, it was fired. Next, it was coated with tin glaze and painted with a design in a metallic pigment such as cobalt or manganese, then fired again. This second firing resulted in a piece that was shiny white except for the painted design. It was coated once again either with a mixture of copper, which gives a golden iridescence, or sulphide of silver. The third and final firing produced a piece that seemed almost to glow.

Hispano-Moresque ware got its name from the mixture of Christian-Spanish and Moorish elements in its decoration, and was made in those parts of Spain that were Muslim or where Muslim artisans were living. Certainly the merest glance at Hispano-Moresque pottery reveals its Near Eastern ancestry: characteristic calligraphic designs, floral patterns and Near Eastern motifs abound. The principal decoration, usually at the center, might be Western—a coat of arms, for example;

Colorplate 7.
Service de l'accouchée, the equivalent of a modern breakfast-in-bed set. Made of tin-glazed earthenware and decorated in enamel colors and gilding, the set reflects French rococo influence. Italian, Milan or Pesaro, c. 1760. Diameter of largest stand: 23.2 cm. (9⅛ in.). Unmarked. Cooper-Hewitt Museum, gift of Norvin Hewitt Green

16.
Hispano-Moresque lustered plate with the arms of Joan Payo Coello, Abbot of Poblet, near Tarragona. Spanish, Manises, Province of Valencia, c. 1480–90. Diameter: 46 cm. (18 in.). Unmarked. Hispanic Society of America

17.
White tin-glazed female figure symbolizing Asia, seated on a camel. From a set of the Four Continents. Spanish, Alcora, last quarter of the eighteenth century. Height: 23.7 cm. (9⅜ in.). Unmarked. Cooper-Hewitt Museum, gift of the Trustees of the Estate of James Hazen Hyde

but this would be surrounded by designs that were clearly of Near Eastern origin (plate 16).

The products of the Hispano-Moresque industry ranged from tablewares, bowls, ewers, vases and drug jars of various sizes to colorful glazed tiles. The last were used extensively in interiors to form handsome dadoes, generally up to four feet high, as well as decorative frames for doors and windows and even risers for staircases. But for appeal to collectors no form of Hispano-Moresque ware equals the plates and dishes. Typically, these are twelve to twenty inches in diameter, and vary from rather flat dinner plates to deep dishes. Particularly appealing are the heraldic beasts, most commonly the rampant lion that appears as a single figure within a shield.

Hispano-Moresque pottery is associated with certain Spanish towns, notably Malaga on the southern coast, and Manises, a suburb of Valencia, directly opposite Majorca. In Malaga, lustered pottery was produced as early as the thirteenth century and continued in superb profusion for the next two hundred years. Much admired abroad, Malaga ware was exported to France, Italy and England. Manises, in the Kingdom of Aragon, was located in what was then Christian territory, but many potters were undoubtedly Moorish. The pottery made there was similar to that of Malaga and reached its peak in the early to mid-fifteenth century (colorplate 8). Other centers for the production of Hispano-Moresque ware were Barcelona, Toledo and Seville.

Golden pottery fell into somewhat of a decline in the fifteenth century, but the high-quality tin-glazed earthenware and peasant ware that had been made concurrently with Hispano-Moresque work continued unabated. By the sixteenth century the town of Talavera in central Spain was already famous for its blue-and-white and polychrome pottery, decorated typically with figures and scenes from daily life. Tablewares, flowerpots, vases, jars, animal figurines and tiles were among the products of the Talavera potters.

But the most important eighteenth-century factory was at Alcora, in eastern Spain. The manufacture of tin-glazed pottery of high quality with polychrome decoration began there in about 1727. Tablewares were the chief products, many decorated with chinoiseries, although figurines (plate 17), portrait busts, vases and other forms were also made until the end of the century. Alcora pottery was seldom marked (when it was, the letter A was incised or painted on), but potters and decorators did sign many of their own pieces.

Colorplate 8.
Hispano-Moresque *brasero*, a dish for holding hot coals, decorated in blue and copper
luster with various abstract designs, including simulated Arabic. Spanish, Manises,
Province of Valencia, c. 1420–30. Diameter:
46 cm. (18 in.). Unmarked. Metropolitan
Museum of Art, New York, Cloisters
Collection

18.
Two Italian maiolica *albarelli*, or drug jars. The example on the left shows a running dog and bears an inscription that reads in translation: "Leave me alone and do not touch me." The one on the right is decorated with deep blue peacocks. Italian, Faenza, c. 1480. Height of the taller jar: 30.5 cm. (12 in.). Unmarked. Metropolitan Museum of Art, New York, Fletcher Fund, 1946

Portugal Neighboring Portugal also has a long ceramic tradition, yet wares from that country have never attracted as much attention as those from Spain. In the eighteenth century, particularly interesting tin-glazed earthenware was made at various centers, among them Aveiro and Coimbra. Tiles, for indoor and outdoor use, were the most successful. Because of Portugal's long connection with the China trade, blue-and-white decoration is common on these pieces. In fact the term *azulejos*, used today for both Portuguese and earlier Spanish tiles, may have been derived from the Spanish word for blue and has frequently been employed to describe such eighteenth-century wares.

Italy The Italians greatly admired the Hispano-Moresque wares of Spain, which were imported into Italy in large numbers during the fifteenth century. Because these wares were apparently shipped from the Iberian mainland via the island of Majorca, Italian importers erroneously assumed they had been made on Majorca, and called them maiolica after their presumed place of origin.

Soon the Italian artisans themselves were emulating Hispano-Moresque wares. Although the art of using tin glaze had been known in Italy as early as the twelfth century—and was probably introduced from the Near East during the Crusades—it was the direct inspiration of the Spanish wares in this medium that launched one of the great periods of Italian ceramics. At first Italian potters copied the essentially medieval Hispano-Moresque style, but they swiftly began to

19.
Maiolica ewer used for liquid drugs. The inscription, translated into English, reads: "Syrup of poppies," a favorite sleeping draft in the medieval pharmacopoeia. Italian, Florence or Faenza, c. 1460–80. Height: 28.6 cm. (11¼ in.). Unmarked. Metropolitan Museum of Art, New York, Fletcher Fund, 1946

imbue their ceramics with a vitality and individual personality that reflected the spirit of the Renaissance at its peak in Italy at this time. Although Italian maiolica was produced from the fifteenth century onward, the earlier wares of the Renaissance period are considered among the finest and have been the most frequently imitated. Admired for five hundred years, this pottery still attracts very strong interest today. It is widely collected.

Maiolica was made in various towns in Italy. Pieces are customarily categorized by the name of the town of their origin. Among the best known of these are Faenza, Urbino, Cafaggiolo, Castel Durante, Gubbio and Venice. Lustered maiolica dates to the beginning of the sixteenth century, and was first made at Deruta in Umbria. Italian lusters were made of either silver, which produces a yellowish sheen, or copper, which results in a ruby red glow. Sometimes an additional thin lead glaze was added as a protective covering.

Although plates and dishes are the most common forms of maiolica, another highly characteristic item much sought by collectors for its decorative appeal is the drug jar. This form originated during the devastating plagues of the Middle Ages, when drug containers—known as *albarelli*—were needed in quantity for monastic pharmacies and noble households. The narrow-waisted ones were used for holding dry drugs and herbs (plate 18). There are also wet drug jars, which have a spout (plate 19). Both kinds are often inscribed with the titles of various drugs and herbs, as well as personal names and mottoes.

20.
Dark blue, tin-glazed earthenware charcoal-burning stove. Italian, eighteenth century. Height: 91 cm. (35½ in.). Unmarked. Cooper-Hewitt Museum, gift of Mrs. Henry E. Huntington

A rather extensive palette was available to painters of maiolica—black, white, blue, yellow, green, purple and orange—and as a result most maiolica ware is very brightly colored. The earliest decorations consisted of geometric designs and plant motifs, reflecting their derivation from the Hispano-Moresque. But by the early sixteenth century maiolica painters had begun to decorate their wares with scenes from stories. This style was therefore known as *istoriato* (literally, "storied") painting. Inspiration was taken from the Bible (*The Presentation of the Virgin* and *Judith and Her Maidservant* are two examples), as well as from the writers of ancient Greece and Rome (see frontispiece). Typical plates and dishes are crowded with figures depicting religious, historical and mythological episodes.

By the middle of the sixteenth century *istoriato* painting had begun to decline, superseded by a new type of maiolica ware characterized by a thick white glaze. Although this ware still carried some polychrome painting, decoration became less important and form took on new significance. Called *bianchi*, it originated in Faenza.

20

The tradition of tin-glazed earthenware continued in Italy through-out the eighteenth century and even later (plates 20–21 and colorplate 7). Many factories that made porcelain, such as those of Doccia near Florence and Le Nove at Venice, also made tin-glazed earthenware. This pottery does not resemble the maiolica of the fifteenth and six-teenth centuries, however, except that it is also tin-glazed earthenware. The white glaze is more prominent, and the less lavish decoration, in monotone and polychrome, includes flowers, chinoiserie and senti-mental views of ruins.

The later maiolica was very actively collected in many parts of Europe and America during the second half of the nineteenth century, when it was popularly called *Raffaele* ware because some of Raphael's paintings were copied in the medium. At the same time the manu-facture of the earlier type of maiolica was revived in Italy, and occasional forgeries were made as well.

21.
Two vertical tile panels, each composed of fifteen individual tiles of tin-glazed enameled earthenware, showing trompe l'oeil curtained balconies with landscape scenes. Italian, Venice (?), eighteenth century. Dimensions of each panel: 64.5 x 38.8 cm. (25⅜ x 15¼ in.). Unmarked. Cooper-Hewitt Museum, gift of the Misses Hewitt

6   French Pottery

The art of making tin-glazed pottery moved north from Italy to France in the early 1500s. There it became known as faience, taking its name from Faenza, the Italian city that was one of the principal manufacturing centers for maiolica.

The first French wares, made at Lyons, Rouen, Nevers and other centers—sometimes by emigrant Italian workmen—were almost indistinguishable from their Italian models and were therefore called French maiolica. Heavy ornate vases, tiles and typically Italian drug jars were popular forms; the resemblance to the Italian style even included decoration with *istoriato* painting and blue and yellow designs surrounding portrait heads.

But by the seventeenth century, French tin-glazed pottery had begun to develop into a new and distinctive art form under the leadership of a succession of brilliant individual craftsmen whose factories turned out tin-glazed pottery of remarkable quality and variety. Given an enormous impetus by government edicts of the late seventeenth and early eighteenth centuries ordering the melting down of gold and silver tablewares to help pay for Louis XIV's extravagant wars, this type of pottery—now known as faience—reached its peak in the eighteenth century. Sets of tablewares predominate, of course, but other popular forms include charming figurines, inkstands, ornate wall fountains (plate 22), ewers, potpourri containers, food warmers and even small, oval chamberpots used by ladies (plate 23). These were called *bourdalous* after the seventeenth-century Jesuit preacher Louis Bourdaloue, whose sermons at Versailles were so popular that ladies arrived hours in advance, often with chamberpots concealed in their muffs, to be assured of a place.

Faience is usually identified by its city of origin and frequently also by the specific factory or workshop that made it. Marks are quite

Colorplate 9.
Faience dog by Émile Gallé, with polychrome overglaze painting and glass eyes. French, Nancy, c. 1870–80. Height: 31.1 cm. (12¼ in.). Mark: signed *E. Gallé, Nancy.* Cooper-Hewitt Museum, anonymous gift

22

common on eighteenth- and even seventeenth-century faience, but rather than being factory marks they are likely to be the initials, monograms or full names of the potters. Reproductions and fakes are equally common, posing a real problem for collectors.

The first great individual name in the history of French ceramics is that of Bernard Palissy, a colorful eccentric whose life story is somewhat shrouded in mystery but who is believed to have been born in 1510 and to have lived to about the age of eighty, his life thus spanning nearly the entire sixteenth century. Originally a glass painter, he was reputedly so taken by the beauty of a single piece of pottery (of unknown origin) that he resolved to devote himself entirely to the study of glazes. A favorite story goes that he experimented so diligently with a kiln requiring immense quantities of wood that he gradually burned up all the furniture in his house and finally the floors! His zeal was rewarded, however, for his pottery became famous for its extraordinarily lush colored glazes, and his whites indicate that he began to make his glazes opaque by using tin—an essential step in making faience.

By the 1550s Palissy was getting commissions, notably from the Montmorency family, to make garden grottoes of glazed pottery that included animals, reptiles and insects, and he showed a weird preference for serpents, toads, frogs and lizards. During a visit to his workshop in Saintes, Catherine de Medici saw one of his commissioned "grottes rustiques" and wanted it for the Tuileries gardens. She persuaded Palissy to move to Paris in about 1556. There he made plates—many of them in the shape of oval ponds—and ewers of the same lead-glazed earthenware decorated in high relief with the same fauna, as well as various examples of marine and amphibious life. The molds for these figures, which are extremely lifelike, may have been made by pouring liquid plaster over real specimens. Although animal forms are the most typical, some of Palissy's dishes have human figures, either allegorical or mythological (plate 24).

An ardent Protestant, Palissy allowed his workshop to be used as a Huguenot meeting place and was frequently in trouble with the religious authorities. Even though his noble patrons protected him, and once prevented his execution, he was finally arrested in 1588 and is believed to have died in a dungeon in 1589 or 1590.

Palissy wares have been forged on a huge scale, but there were also legitimate imitators. In Tours, the Avisseau family flourished during the nineteenth century making dishes, ewers and plates swarming with reptiles and painted and glazed in the Palissy manner. All the forgeries and imitations have confused the collecting of Palissy ware. Without signatures, judgment must be based on appearance and, owing to the excellence of some of the imitations, this can be quite difficult.

22.
Rococo faience wall fountain with cover and basin. At the top, a small figure is perched on a huge seashell, a typical rococo motif; below, a protruding dragon head serves as a spigot. French, Marseilles, c. 1760. Height of fountain: 59.4 cm. (23⅜ in.). Width of basin: 29 cm. (11⅜ in.). Unmarked. Cooper-Hewitt Museum, bequest of Erskine Hewitt

23.
Faience *bourdalou* (ladies' chamberpot), with polychrome floral decoration on a white background. French, Aprey, eighteenth century. Overall length: 22.5 cm. (8⅞ in.). Unmarked. Cooper-Hewitt Museum, gift of Mr. and Mrs. Maxime Hermanos

24.
Oval dish of lead-glazed earthenware attributed to Bernard Palissy. Four buff-colored cherubs with blue wings appear in molded relief against mottled blue and brown background between decorative medallions. French, late sixteenth century. Overall length: 33.3 cm. (13 in.). Unmarked. Cooper-Hewitt Museum, gift of Robert Lehman

23

24

Mention should be made, too, of the famous pottery known as St. Porchaire, or Henri II, ware, also made in the sixteenth century. Unlike faience, this refined pottery was made of a clay that, even when fired, was of a pure white color; decoration consisted of intricate colored lines in complex patterns that have been compared to tooled bookbindings. The white body of the wares required no tin glaze; instead a basic clear lead glaze was used to cover the surfaces of the wares.

While Palissy was creating his idiosyncratic yet advanced glazed wares, the mainstream of French tin-glazed earthenware manufacture was gathering momentum, and important pottery centers emerged.

25

26

The city of Rouen was one of the earliest faience-making centers. Its wares are associated with factories run by several generations of the Poterat family. The first of this dynasty was Edmé Poterat, who obtained a fifty-year monopoly for the manufacture of pottery in Normandy in 1644; one son succeeded him, and another, Louis, opened a rival factory nearby. Rouen faience of the seventeenth century was inspired by Chinese porcelain and Dutch Delft; using these two types as models, the Poterats evolved a ware that was initially decorated largely in blue-and-white.

In the early eighteenth century, toward the end of the reign of Louis XIV, craftsmen in Rouen began to employ decorative motifs called *lambrequins*—scalloped border patterns reminiscent of the ornate baroque drapery festoons found on windows and fourposter beds of the time. Usually consisting of alternating large and small motifs, lambrequins frequently radiated from the center of the design in what is known as the *style rayonnant*, a tribute perhaps to the Sun King. Popular from about 1690 to 1740, this style was first executed in blue-and-white, and later in polychrome painting. The polychrome palette of Rouen was restricted to those colors able to take high-temperature firing—1100 to 1450 degrees Celsius. The red glowed particularly well, contributing greatly to the success of Rouen wares in the eighteenth century. Polychrome rococo designs, consisting of cockleshells, garlands, pastoral scenes, cupids and flowers, and chinoiserie

25.
Heart-shaped faience inkstand decorated in blue-and-white with conventionalized flowers and foliage. French, Rouen, c. 1780. Overall length: 15.8 cm. (6¼ in.). Unmarked. Cooper-Hewitt Museum, gift of the Misses Hewitt

26.
Faience baby's cap stand with underglaze decoration painted with blue and mauve chinoiseries. French, Nevers, late seventeenth–eighteenth century. Height: 11 cm. (4¼ in.). Unmarked. Cooper-Hewitt Museum, bequest of Richard Cranch Greenleaf, in memory of his mother, Adeline Emma Greenleaf

motifs such as mandarins, pagodas and dragons, followed after 1740.

Rouen faience was made in an immense variety of forms: these ranged from small objects—inkstands (plate 25), spice boxes and salt-cellars, often modeled after silverware—to enormous dishes (some up to two feet in diameter) and even six-foot globes, examples of which still survive. Rouen had eleven factories employing over two thousand workmen in 1722, and eighteen factories by 1783; its techniques, shapes and designs spread to many other pottery centers in France.

Another early center was the city of Nevers in central France. Nevers at first adopted the Italian "pictorial style" of decoration, which was popular until about 1650. Taken from engravings by such artists as Nicolas Poussin and Sir Anthony Van Dyck, these illustrations were executed on large faience dishes in both blue-and-white and polychrome colors. During the seventeenth century Nevers wares increasingly showed blue and pale purple decoration (a later example is shown in plate 26) in imitation of Chinese wares. And in the latter half of that century, the city became famous for its *bleu persan*, or Persian blue, backgrounds—wares ornamented in white or light colors. Large numbers of popular pieces in the form of plates, bottles and jugs

27.
Ceramic cooling pails were used in eighteenth-century France to chill bottles of wine. This example is tin-glazed earthenware with blue overglaze decoration in classical motifs, featuring a geometric border at the bottom, a foliate or arabesque border around the top and an urn topped by swags in the center. French, Moustiers, mideighteenth century. Height: 21 cm. (8¼ in.). Unmarked. Cooper-Hewitt Museum, gift of George A. Hearn

carrying inscriptions of dates or personal names were made for special occasions during the eighteenth century and were known as *faïences parlantes*; similar objects containing pictures of name saints, known as *faïences patronymes*, were popular as birthday gifts. Nevers remained active during the French Revolution, producing *faïences patriotiques* bearing all sorts of nationalistic emblems and sayings. Its factories were still making faience well into the nineteenth century.

Moustiers, a town about sixty miles northeast of Marseilles, emerged as a pottery center in the 1670s when Pierre Clérissy, who is said to have learned how to make tin-glazed pottery from an Italian monk, opened a factory there. He was the first of a large family of potters who remained active in the area until the middle of the nineteenth century. Early Moustiers wares were decorated with lively paintings, especially hunting scenes copied from the engravings of the Florentine painter Antonio Tempesta and executed in blue. Other subjects were mythological and biblical scenes showing figures dressed in Louis XIV costume.

During the first half of the eighteenth century, Moustiers ware was dominated by what is known as the *style bérain*, which consisted of airy, interlaced designs incorporating assorted classical motifs such as urns and garlands (plate 27), sphinxes, satyrs and nymphs. These were taken from the works of Jean Bérain, costume and set designer for Louis XIV's masques and operas. After 1740, typical rococo decorations were introduced. Designs after the engravings of Jacques Callot, notably his grotesques featuring fantastic animals, were especially popular.

Nearby Marseilles was a major manufacturing center for faience, beginning in the latter part of the seventeenth century when Joseph Clérissy, brother of Pierre, opened a factory in 1679 that produced wares similar to those of Moustiers. Among other Marseilles factories, that of Pierrette Caudelot, the widow of Claude Perrin, is outstanding. Madame Perrin took over the factory established by her husband from the time of his death in 1748 until her own in 1793. She was by no means the only woman to run a factory in her own name, but the quality of her production, mainly tablewares (colorplate 10), sets her firm apart. The painting on Veuve (Widow) Perrin rococo faience is free and naturalistic rather than studied, which gives her pieces an air of charming simplicity. Figurines, again intended mostly as table decorations, were also made. Collectors are devoted to the Veuve Perrin wares, which are often marked *VP*.

Alsace-Lorraine boasted a whole series of faience factories in the eighteenth century, of which Strasbourg is probably the most famous. Early in the century Charles-François Hannong (originally Carl Franz, a Dutchman) started to manufacture faience there in partnership with a potter from the famous German firm of Meissen, and later Han-

Colorplate 10.
Faience tureen with cover from the factory of the widow of Claude Perrin, combining polychrome chinoiserie scenes with whimsical handles in the shape of leopards and a fish. French, Marseilles, 1750–70. Length: 40.5 cm. (16 in.). Unmarked. Cooper-Hewitt Museum, gift of Eleanor Garnier Hewitt

Colorplate 11.
Tureen with cover in the form of a pigeon.
Faience. French, Strasbourg, Paul Hannong
period, c. 1750–60. Length: 33.5 cm. (13¼
in). Unmarked. Metropolitan Museum of
Art, New York, gift of R. Thornton Wilson,
1950, in memory of Florence Ellsworth
Wilson

28.
Jardiniere on stand in glazed, high-fired
earthenware. The floral relief decoration is
blue, purple and green against a red ground.
French, c. 1890. Overall height: 79 cm. (31
in.). Mark: pseudo-Japanese. Cooper-Hewitt
Museum, bequest of Cornelie J. Oppenheim

28

nong's son Paul succeeded him. Under Paul's direction, beginning in 1738, Strasbourg faience became the first to be decorated with the same full range of colors used on porcelain. This was achieved by painting the decorations after the glaze had been fired at a high temperature and fixing the colors to the glaze by firing again at a much lower temperature (700–900 degrees Celsius). Previously only one firing was used so that faience colors had been restricted to those few that could withstand the very high temperatures needed to fire the glaze. Strasbourg wares are usually very ornate. Tureens in animal and bird shapes were a specialty (colorplate 11).

At Niderviller in Lorraine, the techniques of Strasbourg were followed but understated. Flower painting in the rococo style was of a very high order, as was the painting of miniature landscapes and figures taken from the works of Antoine Watteau and François Boucher. Niderviller also produced many fine figurines from the 1750s to the 1780s.

By the close of the eighteenth century the great age of French faience was in decline, partly as a result of the trauma of the French Revolution, but also because of competition from English firms, which were sending large quantities of so-called creamware into the European markets. This beautiful cream-colored earthenware with its transparent lead glaze was deliberately created by Josiah Wedgwood and others to compete with porcelain. To meet the English challenge, manufacture of creamware was established in France at several places—Paris, Lunéville, Chantilly and Creil, among others—under the name *faïence fine*.

From the 1840s on, traditional French potters were caught up in the revival of historic styles (plate 28) that swept over all the decorative arts in Europe at that time. They were therefore more anxious to develop the styles and techniques of the past than to explore new forms of pottery. But simultaneously work on new designs by individual artists began, and France can lay claim to producing the first internationally known artist-potter, Théodore Deck (1825–1891), who began to make earthenware of his own design in 1856. A great student of Near Eastern wares, especially those of Turkey and Iran, and of Chinese traditions of pottery making, Deck was strongly influenced too by the later nineteenth-century fondness for Japanese art and culture. He was particularly intrigued by glazes, and created exquisite faience with motifs derived from various Oriental pottery styles (colorplate 12).

Colorplate 12.
Glazed pottery dish by Théodore Deck—
one of the first of the artist-potters to gain
international recognition—who was director
of the Sèvres Manufactory at the time it was
made. French, Sèvres, c. 1885. Diameter:
49.8 cm. (19½ in.). Marks: *H Deck*. Cooper-
Hewitt Museum, gift of Eleanor Garnier
Hewitt

Deck had many followers; by the last years of the nineteenth century an entire generation of French artist-potters was creating ceramics of different types. At this point, the Art Nouveau movement was at its height, and these artists were influenced by its fluid, sinuous lines, derived to some extent from Japanese styles.

Among the most famous artist-potters of this group was Ernest Chaplet, who made extraordinarily fine glazed stoneware based on Chinese models of the Sung dynasty; known as *flambé* glaze, this style of decoration consisted of brilliant red and purple streaks. Chaplet also fired pottery for his friend, the painter Gauguin, who tried unsuccessfully to augment his income by modeling pottery by hand between sojourns in Martinique and Tahiti. After Théodore Deck, probably the best-known individual figure of this era—especially to collectors—is Émile Gallé (1846–1904) of Nancy, admired as a designer in many fields, particularly glass. Like so many other artist-potters, Gallé was extremely interested in glazes for ceramics, above all the Japanese drip glazes. He is noted too for his earthenware animals (see colorplate 9), and today his work is much admired.

In 1925, a new international style, later to be called Art Deco, was launched as a result of an exhibition held in Paris—the Exposition Internationale des Arts Décoratifs et Industriels Modernes. Essentially, Art Deco attempted to bridge the gap between industry and art by eliminating detail and by stressing strong, bold shapes and colors and geometric designs such as zigzags and circles. Ceramics played a large role in the entire Art Deco movement of the 1920s and 1930s, and some of the potters most active in Art Nouveau also worked in the new style.

Émile Decoeur was one of the key names of the Art Deco era in France. An experimenter in ceramics, he took the unusual approach of painting decorations on stoneware; later in his career Decoeur usually settled for superb matte glazes without any other surface decoration. Émile Lenoble (who was Ernest Chaplet's stepson and trained by him) was another important French potter in the era between the wars. His work was typically characterized by incised motifs—both geometric and stylized floral—that revealed the gray ground of the wares. Outstanding too was René Buthaud, a painter whose pottery was usually decorated with animal and human figures (plate 29). These men had many colleagues and followers—and the Art Deco ceramics of France include pieces of remarkable quality (colorplate 13).

Twentieth-century painters working in France have been extremely interested in ceramics, which they often decorate and sign. Pablo Picasso is one of the most important of these (plate 30). Joan Miró, who worked closely with the Spanish potter José Llorens Artigas in France, is another.

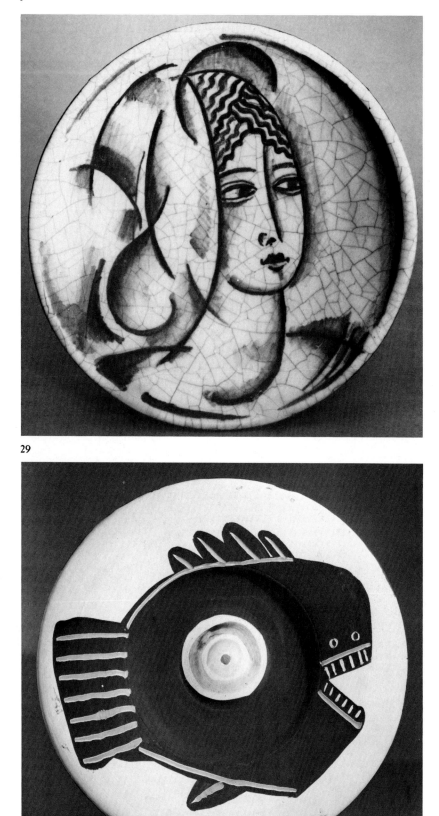

29

30

29.
Faience dish with matte-gray crackle glaze, decorated in the Art Deco style with the face of a woman wearing a large hat, by René Buthaud. French, c. 1925–30. Diameter: 20.5 cm. (8 in.). Mark: signed with cipher "*RB*" in black. Smithsonian Institution, National Museum of American History

30.
Pablo Picasso decorated a number of ceramic pieces while living in the south of France, late in his career. This earthenware plate was painted with a design he called *Le Gros Poisson Noir* on a stock shape from the Poterie Madoura. French, Vallauris, 1957. Diameter: 43.5 cm. (17 in.). Mark: artist's signature and date *16.4.1957*. Cooper-Hewitt Museum, gift of Mr. and Mrs. Daniel Saidenberg

Colorplate 13.
Art Deco-style statue entitled *Homme Vainqueur de ses Passions*, by Willy Wuilleumier, a Swiss potter who worked in Paris, showing a man on a horse attacking a stylized monster. Glazed earthenware, with walnut base (a later addition). French, Fau & Guillard, c. 1924. Overall length: 50.5 cm. (19¾ in.). Cooper-Hewitt Museum, from the collection of the late Stanley Siegel, gift of Stanley Siegel

7 The Pottery of Northern Europe

While the art of creating maiolica ware was at a peak in Italy, and France was just beginning to develop an individual style of tin-glazed pottery, Germany made a very important contribution to the history of ceramics in the form of salt-glazed stoneware. Throughout most of the sixteenth century the great pottery centers of the Rhineland produced and exported an extraordinary variety of jugs, beakers, tankards, plates and other forms in this medium, often ornately decorated in low relief and generally known as Rhenish ware.

Gradually the technique of making tin-glazed pottery moved north to Germany and the Low Countries, and eventually to Scandinavia. Early northern tin-glazed pottery is usually referred to as German maiolica and Dutch maiolica because of its close resemblance to Italian wares. But in the seventeenth and eighteenth centuries northern faience developed into a distinctive style, strongly influenced everywhere by the work of the brilliant Delft potters and then by the exquisite Chinese porcelains being imported in quantity at that time.

The production of salt-glazed stoneware declined as the popularity of faience increased. Tin-glazed pottery remained dominant in northern Europe until it was superseded, as in France, by the huge influx of British creamware that began in the late eighteenth century.

Stoneware As a pottery type, stoneware is related to porcelain, being hard, nonporous and resonant; but unlike porcelain, it is not translucent. Very high temperatures (1200 to 1400 degrees Celsius) are needed to produce stoneware. This fact probably accounts for the German preeminence in the medium, since in late medieval times large amounts of wood were required for the tremendous kiln fires to achieve such temperatures, and Germany was then very heavily forested.

Colorplate 14.
The potteries of the Cologne area were a distinguished source of Bellarmines, salt-glazed stoneware wine jugs decorated with representations of bearded men. German, Frechen, late sixteenth century. Height: 36.8 cm. (14½ in.). Metropolitan Museum of Art, New York, Rogers Fund, 1910

31.
German jug of the Bellarmine type, in brown salt-glazed stoneware with three medallions on belly. Germany, Frechen, late sixteenth century. Height: 21.6 cm. (8½ in.). Mark: string mark on base. Smithsonian Institution, National Museum of American History

The German stoneware was glazed with salt, which was simply thrown into the kiln when the heat was at its greatest. The sodium in the salt combined with elements in the clay to form a glaze. This salt glaze produced a thin, colorless, slightly pebbled surface that has often been compared to the skin of an orange; brown pottery with a special mottled appearance is known as tigerware. Not many colors were possible because of the intense heat of the firing: salt-glazed ware is usually white, gray or brown, and occasionally off-white.

The earliest of the great Rhineland stoneware centers to achieve prominence was Cologne, which began to turn out exceptional wares beginning in about 1525. Here the gray stoneware was covered with a slip wash that ranged in color from dark chestnut brown to a dull yellow, with an overall speckled effect. The city is most famous for its wine containers, called *Bartmannkrüge*: literally, "bearded-man jugs."

Decorated with the mask of a bearded man on the short neck of the vessel, these jugs were used to export Rhine wine to England. There they became known as Graybeards, or Bellarmines, because of a seeming resemblance between the mask and Cardinal Roberto Bellarmino (1542–1621). He was an Italian Catholic prelate who wrote a number of books against the Protestant movement, so the name, in Protestant countries at least, was intended as a slight. In the late sixteenth century many Cologne potters moved to the nearby town of Frechen, where they continued to make and export Bellarmines (colorplate 14 and plate 31) on a large scale well into the eighteenth century.

Siegburg was another important early stoneware center. Manufacture expanded there from around 1550, and a specialty was a tall, narrow tankard with slightly tapering sides called a *Schnelle* (plate 32), also made at other stoneware factories. Typically, these were adorned with biblical subjects encased in medallions or in three rows of low relief. *Schnellen* and other vessels, such as jugs, wine bottles and pitchers, were often provided with metal mounts.

The greatest of the Rhenish stoneware centers was at Raeren, near Aix-la-Chapelle. Its supremacy was due to the work of Jan Emens Mennicken, generally known as Jan Emens and perhaps the most famous single maker of German stoneware. Beginning in about 1566, Emens produced huge jugs decorated with biblical and mythological subjects such as Susanna and the Elders, the Judgment of Paris and the Battle of the Centaurs, frequently taken from engravings. These busy relief decorations were characteristically separated by horizontal bands, giving a fine sense of structure and an almost architectural feeling to his work. Emens's early wares were dark brown, the later ones gray decorated with cobalt blue. He signed his pieces with his initials and sometimes the date; however, members of his family, who carried on his work after his death, used his models and the same marks. Farther down the Rhine, in the Westerwald region, several towns produced a white ware similar to that of Siegburg, and in the latter part of the sixteenth century a gray-colored stoneware with painted blue decoration, much of which was intended for foreign markets.

By the second decade of the seventeenth century the great age of Rhenish stoneware was beginning to draw to a close. Its decline was hastened by the advent of the Thirty Years' War (1618–48), when much of Germany was devastated by armies of many nationalities. Both Raeren and Siegburg were sacked, their stoneware industries ruined. Experts believe that some of the potters fled, taking with them the molds for the pottery, which was later reproduced in other parts of the country. We know that stoneware production resumed in the second half of the seventeenth century. Wares ranged from Westerwald pottery in the north, decorated for export with English coats of arms, to jars and tankards painted with brilliantly colored overglaze

32.
Siegburg stoneware tankard with pewter mount. The relief medallions depict scenes from the lives of Joseph, Joshua and David. Germany, Siegburg, late sixteenth century. Height: 34.3 cm. (13½ in.). Unmarked. Cooper-Hewitt Museum, purchased in memory of Georgiana L. McClellan

enamel in the south, at Kreussen in Bavaria (plate 33). Many centers continued production well into the nineteenth century.

It should be stressed that the dates often found on stoneware cannot be taken as actual years of production since these later centers held to traditional styles and frequently used the same molds for generations. "Early" pieces were also extensively forged in the nineteenth century to meet collectors' demands.

Hafner Ware   Italian potters crossed the Alps in the sixteenth century. Their influence was seen in the early 1500s in Nuremberg, where craftsmen, known as *Hafneren* (literally, "stove-makers"), were producing lead-glazed green ceramic tiles—decorated with ornate relief molding—to be used on stoves. Gradually, under the leadership of Hafner Paul Preuning, these workers began to decorate their reliefs in strong polychrome colors similar to those in Italian tin-glazed pieces. Nuremberg also produced highly ornate maiolica wares, particularly lidded jugs in the shape of an owl.

Maiolica   Antwerp became the first major center for maiolica ware in the Low Countries. As early as 1512 an Italian potter from Castel Durante, Guido Andries (or di Savino), was working there, and he and his family helped to spread the art. By about 1600 maiolica was being produced in Rotterdam, Amsterdam, Haarlem and other Netherlands towns. Utilitarian articles of various kinds were made, including tableware, ointment pots and drug jars; decorative tiles were also among the major products of all these potteries. Today, the origin of these pieces can seldom be precisely identified.

The Dutch maiolica was not nearly as sophisticated as that of Italy. Its finish was cruder, and its colors more garish. The decoration was geometrical, or portrayed figures such as horsemen or milkmaids; a few pieces had designs copied from Chinese inscriptions. Some carried inscriptions or injunctions from the Bible.

Delftware   Dutch maiolica was replaced by a new style in the seventeenth century, when Delftware—which is also tin-glazed earthenware but usually with Chinese models rather than Italian—began to be made in quantity. During the nineteenth century, as part of the great revival of interest in all early ceramics, Dutch Delftware was reproduced on a large scale.

Dutch Delftware takes its name from the town of Delft in the Netherlands, one of the most important centers for its manufacture; but the pottery now called by that name was actually also made at many other places in the Low Countries. Delft-type pottery was made in England too under the same name (but generally termed delft or delftware without the initial capital *D*).

The Dutch East India Company provided the inspiration for this

33.
Enameled stoneware jar with silver-gilt screw top and mount. German, Bavaria, possibly Kreussen, c. 1675. Height: 22.3 cm. (8¾ in.). Marks: *FO* on mount for Franz Oxner and angel indicating Munich. Cooper-Hewitt Museum, gift of Milton J. Blume

Colorplate 15.
Delft figure of a cow, executed in tin-enameled earthenware with polychrome decoration. Dutch, eighteenth century. Height: 9.5 cm. (3¾ in.). Metropolitan Museum of Art, New York, gift of Henry G. Marquand, 1894

new style of pottery by importing large quantities of Chinese porcelains in the early 1600s. Attempting to emulate porcelain, the Delft potters tried a more refined clay than had been used for maiolica ware and added an extra glaze to achieve a glossier finish. First the buff-colored clay was shaped and fired; then it was dipped in white tin enamel and decorated. After being painted, it was covered with a transparent lead glaze (*kwaart*) and fired again, very carefully, to achieve a smooth, shiny surface.

Decoration of Delft ran to landscapes, portraits, rural scenes, biblical episodes, religious inscriptions, patriotic slogans and, as might be expected, imitation of the birds and flowers shown on late Ming and early Ch'ing porcelain. While the majority of pieces favored blue-and-white in imitation of Chinese wares, some were produced in white, undecorated; others were gilded (Delft *doré*) or painted on a black ground (Delft *noire*). In the eighteenth century some polychrome ware was also produced in imitation of Japanese and Chinese decoration and of the French rococo style.

All types of tablewares, decorative plates (plate 34), drug and tobacco jars, jugs, cruets, sets of vases, flowerpots, boxes, pickle trays, chess sets, candlesticks, birdcages and figurines (colorplate 15) were among the Delft products. Particularly famous are the blue-and-white Delft tiles made to decorate walls and fireplaces. The subject matter of these tiles was even more varied: marine scenes, biblical stories, landscapes, harbor scenes and thousands of other subjects, sometimes painted in colors.

Delftware is frequently marked, in a bewildering variety, by factories, owners, potters, decorators. Identifiable Delft factories with marks have curious names, such as De Metale Pot (The Metal Pot), De Dubbele Schenkkan (The Double Jug), De Paauw (The Peacock), De Grieksche A (The Greek A), De Drie Klokken (The Three Bells). This is partly because after 1654 the potters at Delft took over the buildings—and names—of defunct breweries. Among the potters, one of the most important families was that of the Eenhoorns, who were active from about the middle of the seventeenth century to around 1773.

From the mid-seventeenth to the end of the eighteenth century Delftware was produced in enormous amounts. The peak period, according to most authorities, was 1670–1730; but the glossy surface and skillful painting of this highly finished ware made it popular all over Europe for nearly two centuries, in all its traditional forms (plate 35).

34.

34.
Delft plate decorated in blue-and-white chinoiserie. Dutch, c. 1700. Diameter: 34.2 cm. (13½ in.). Mark: pseudo-Chinese character in blue. Smithsonian Institution, National Museum of American History, Dr. Hans Syz Collection

35.
Delft birdcage with finely detailed blue-and-white scenic paintings depicting landscapes and seascapes on all sides. Dutch, probably Delft, c. 1830. Height: 26.7 cm. (10½ in.). Unmarked. Cooper-Hewitt Museum, gift of the Misses Hewitt

35

36

36.
Tin-glazed earthenware stove tile with under-glaze blue decoration. It has a heavy baroque border painted to suggest an aperture in a wall through which one views a delicately shaded landscape scene. German, possibly Hamburg, eighteenth century. Length: 34.2 cm. (13½ in.). Width: 15.8 cm. (6¼ in.). Cooper-Hewitt Museum, gift of Henry Frederick William Rave

37.
Plate (opposite page, inset) from a famous Polish delft service presented by King Stanislas Poniatowski to Sultan Abdul Hamid I of Turkey. The decoration is of the Imari (Japanese) type with an inscription in Turkish saluting the sultan. Polish, Warsaw, Belvedere factory, c. 1774–89. Diameter: 34.6 cm. (13½ in.). Unmarked. Smithsonian Institution, National Museum of American History, gift of Alfred Duane Pell Fund

Faience Emigrant workmen from the Low Countries established the first important German faience factory at Hanau in the 1660s. The early wares have great similarity to Dutch Delftware, but Hanau pottery is heavier and slightly coarser. Most connoisseurs also feel that the painting lacks the skill of the Dutch painters and the finish is not so brilliant. Hanau produced a great many pieces as tablewares for middle-class households. The painted decoration in a pattern known as *Vögelesdekor* (literally, "bird decoration"), which consists of exotic birds, flowers and groups of dots, was characteristic.

The faience factory at Frankfurt-am-Main, established about the same time as Hanau's, aimed higher, producing richer wares, many of them intended for display rather than everyday use. Chinoiserie, derived from Delftware, was much employed in the decoration, but there was also a sort of *istoriato* painting, called *historieteller* in Frankfurt, quite like that on Italian maiolica. Some Frankfurt pottery is marked with a capital *F* and the initials of the painter.

Frankfurt, Hanau and other early German faiences were frequently painted by professional decorators who worked independently of the factories. They were known as *Hausmaler*, meaning literally "painters who worked at home," or, in contemporary terms, freelance artists. Because these men were not under factory supervision, the quality of their work varied enormously.

These were the most important early faience factories. During the eighteenth century new potteries were established all over the country, notably at Nuremberg, Höchst, Fulda, Ansbach and Hamburg (plate 36). In all, there were probably as many as eighty faience factories active in eighteenth-century Germany. Their influence spread as far as Poland, where the Belvedere factory in Warsaw produced beautiful pieces in the Chinese style. Most famous, however, is an exquisite service decorated in the Japanese Imari style in blue, red and gold, made for the Sultan of Turkey (plate 37).

In the eighteenth century faience manufacture also moved to the Scandinavian countries of Sweden, Norway and Denmark, although the tradition of peasant pottery—mostly decorated with white slip—was highly developed in Scandinavia at this time and would continue alongside the new style almost to the present day.

Faience factories were established at a number of places in Sweden, the two most prominent being Rörstrand and Marieberg. Rörstrand began operations in the 1720s, making blue-and-white faience very like that of Delft and Rouen; later it was noted for its rococo wares painted in white on a blue-gray background. Large ceramic tea-table trays were made at Rörstrand, in addition to plates, jugs, bowls and so on. Marieberg opened in 1758 under the direction of Johann Ehren-reich, who had connections with the royal court—he had been the king's dentist. The Marieberg faience, generally more elegant than that of Rörstrand, was painted with a brilliant palette of enamels. The factory was sold to Rörstrand in 1782.

In the 1760s and 1770s a fine faience was made in Norway at Herrebøe. It was painted in a particularly exuberant rococo style that has been much admired both for its color and for its deftness of execution.

In Denmark, the Store Kongensgade in Copenhagen made blue-decorated faience almost exclusively. By law it was granted the privilege of being the only Danish factory to use this color, and the importation of blue-painted wares into Denmark was forbidden at the instigation of the owners of the factory. A peculiar product of Store Kongensgade was a punchbowl in the shape of a bishop's miter. Other important Danish manufactories were Kastrup, Østerbro and Mors.

The Modern Movement   By the late nineteenth and early twentieth centuries the same interests that encouraged the French artist-potters to break new ground affected those of northern Europe as well: the

influence of Japanese and Chinese ceramic masterpieces; the Art Nouveau movement, known in German-speaking countries as *Jugendstil*;
and the inspiration derived from pioneering contemporaries.

In Germany during this period fine wares were produced by large
firms interested in reviving ceramics as a real art form in an era of
growing mass production and by experimental studio potters, working
essentially alone. A good example of the latter was Hermann Mutz, who
worked in Altona near Hamburg. By about 1900 he was producing
beautiful stoneware with brown, green or blue drip glazes emulating
Japanese models. In contrast, the large firm of Villeroy and Boch in

38.
Michael Powolny was the maker of this
terra-cotta statue of Neptune, which is
glazed in mottled white. Austrian, Vienna,
probably Wiener Keramik, early twentieth
century. Overall height: 134.6 cm. (52½ in.).
Unmarked. Cooper-Hewitt Museum, from
the collection of the late Stanley Siegel, gift
of Stanley Siegel

Mettlach pioneered the re-creation of fine Rhenish stoneware of the seventeenth century.

In Vienna, the so-called Sezession movement—closely associated with Jugendstil—dominated the arts in the 1880s and inevitably influenced the design of ceramics. Shortly after the turn of the century, experimental workshops for different disciplines, known as Wiener Werkstätte, were established; the one where ceramic artists and craftsmen got together was the Wiener Keramik. Several distinguished potters were associated with this workshop, including Michael Powolny, who became noted for his large, sometimes rather ornamental figurines, both animal and human (plate 38). Equally prominent was Josef Hoffmann, who favored a more severe, functional design and later created outstanding tablewares in the Modern style.

The Bauhaus—the Weimar Art School—which was founded in 1919 and lasted until 1933, was an important advocate of this Modern style. Although the school was interested in promoting the functional approach to architectural design and many other arts, it had a separate pottery workshop with which an important group of artists, including Hoffmann, was associated. Outstanding modern pottery has also been made in the Netherlands by potters working, for example, at the historic De Porseleyne Fles factory in Delft, and in Gouda (plate 39), as well as in individual studios.

39.
Glazed and lustered earthenware bowl in shades of iridescent copper and silver. Dutch, Gouda, 1925–50. Height: 10.9 cm. (4¼ in.). Diameter: 21 cm. (8¼ in.). Marks: *Unique Metallique, Plazvid, Gouda, Holland* and symbols. Cooper-Hewitt Museum, gift of Mrs. Helen Kroll Kramer, in memory of Dr. Milton Lurie Kramer

40.
Modern stoneware jar with light gray *flambé* glaze, speckled with blue. The cover is bronze with a silver butterfly on a circular base. Danish, Copenhagen, Royal Copenhagen Porcelain Factory, 1922. Height: 11 cm. (4⅜ in.). Mark: underglaze blue mark on bottom, three wavy lines and numerals; cover marked with crown, three wavy lines and numerals. Cooper-Hewitt Museum, gift of Mrs. A. Murray Young

Twentieth-century design owes much to Scandinavia. In the late nineteenth century the Scandinavian countries fostered some outstanding artist-potters. Unlike the craftsmen of France and elsewhere, they produced comparatively little stoneware. The two most noted Danish artist-potters are probably Herman A. Kähler of Naestved and Thorvald Bindesbøll. Bindesbøll had a powerful, distinctive style, emphasizing the wavy lines that separate colors inspired (as one commentary put it) "by the clouds of the skies and the waves of the sea." Earthenware vases with ruddy brown or deep blue glazes, sometimes lustered, are typical of Kähler's work.

The ceramic firms themselves have played an important role in establishing modern Scandinavian pottery. As far back as the 1890s, the old Swedish firm of Rörstrand employed artists to design wares in the Art Nouveau style; subtly colored vases with large flowers in relief design are typical. The Royal Copenhagen factory in Denmark took on artist-potters, who worked in the Japanese and Art Nouveau styles, producing interesting stonewares in the 1920s and 1930s (plate 40). Another individualistic Danish factory was the Saxbo pottery, run in the 1930s by Nathalie Krebs, a chemical engineer who was intrigued by stoneware glazes. And since World War I the Finnish firm of Arabia (originally an offshoot of Rörstrand in Sweden) has produced outstanding earthenware and stoneware vases in the Art Nouveau style. More recently, it has developed wares that are heat-resistant, bringing function and beauty to the everyday presentation of food.

8 English Pottery

English native pottery of the early sixteenth century was country work, created locally by individuals for everyday use. A type of lead-glazed earthenware, it was decorated with white slip and is therefore known as slipware. Although such pottery has great charm and was made with considerable skill, interest in more sophisticated wares imported from the Continent began to be felt at about this time. Tin-glazed earthenware, introduced by emigrant Dutch and Flemish potters, soon achieved immense popularity and became known in England as delftware. It was produced in large quantities during the seventeenth and eighteenth centuries. Another import that inspired British manufacture was salt-glazed stoneware from Germany. First produced in England in the latter part of the seventeenth century, it was also in great demand throughout most of the next century.

The production of traditional British lead-glazed wares continued, however, and developed alongside the new. Eventually, in the middle of the eighteenth century, a different form of lead-glazed pottery, known as English creamware, began to replace delft and stoneware not only in England but on the Continent. This unique ware, developed by Josiah Wedgwood and others and produced primarily in Staffordshire and Leeds, was tremendously popular.

Creamware remained dominant in England until the early nineteenth century, but other splendid ceramics in various mediums were also produced in Staffordshire and at various centers during the eighteenth century and throughout the Victorian era. Many of these wares were made not only for British and Continental markets but for export to the newly independent American nation.

Colorplate 16.
Wedgwood plaque of jasperware, depicting the marriage of Cupid and Psyche in black and white. English, Etruria, Josiah Wedgwood, 1769–80. Length: 35.6 cm. (14 in.). Mark: impressed *WEDGWOOD & BENTLEY*. Brooklyn Museum, Emily Winthrop Miles Collection

Delftware From the collector's point of view, the tin-glazed pottery that the English began to make in the sixteenth century marks the first important period of English ceramics. English delftware had a direct line of descent from tin-glazed Italian maiolica. In the late Renaissance maiolica makers emigrated to and taught their craft in the Low Countries, and their techniques crossed the Channel from there. It is not certain when this took place, but there is strong evidence that it occurred in the first half of the sixteenth century. The so-called Malling Jugs (mottled tin-glazed earthenwares named after a piece found at West Malling church in Kent) have silver mounts dated as early as 1549 and are now believed to have been made by Flemish potters working in England, rather than to have been imported.

Recorded evidence begins with the arrival, in 1567, of two Flemish potters, named Jasper Andries and Jacob Jansen, who came from Antwerp and settled in Norwich. They applied for a government license to operate a pottery in 1571. It was granted, and Andries remained in Norwich while Jansen moved to Aldgate in London. They created the earliest documented tin-glazed wares in England and production soon spread to other potteries.

Some seventeenth-century tin-glazed wares were decorated with bold polychrome designs. Characteristic of this style were large shallow dishes—up to sixteen inches in diameter—decorated in brilliant colors; particularly popular after the Restoration of the monarchy in 1660, these were intended not for use but for display on walls and dressers. Typical subjects included royal figures, Adam and Eve and the Tree of Life (plate 41), other biblical scenes, admired military heroes and flowers.

Simultaneously, from the 1620s on, some English potters began to take their inspiration from Chinese models—following the example of the tin-glaze potters of Delft—and to recorate their earthenware in blue-and-white with Chinese-inspired designs. Eventually, this style replaced the earlier polychrome colors. Much English delft of this period also remained undecorated. Because the development of English tin-glazed earthenware paralleled so closely that of Delft, it became known as English delft.

Delftware is classified by its place of production: London, Bristol and Liverpool were the principal centers, but factories existed in other towns, including Dublin and Glasgow. Within these centers, place of origin can sometimes be narrowed. London delft, for example, can be classified as being manufactured in Southwark or Lambeth, both on the south bank of the Thames; one of the potteries at Southwark had the charming address of Pickleherring Stairs. Brislington, a suburb of Bristol, is used as a subclassification of Bristol. A high percentage of delft, however, can be identified only as "English" and cannot be assigned to a specific factory.

The forms of English delft are numerous and intriguing. The usual

41.
Adam and Eve with the serpent and the Tree of Life, shown here in polychrome, was a common motif on English delftware during most of the seventeenth century. English, Lambeth, c. 1665. Diameter: 42.9 cm. (16⅞ in.). Unmarked. Smithsonian Institution, National Museum of American History, Dr. Lloyd E. Hawes Collection

42.
Flower-shaped English delft pickle dish with blue floral decoration. English, probably Bristol, c. 1750–69. Diameter: 16 cm. (6¼ in.). Unmarked. Smithsonian Institution, National Museum of American History, Dr. Lloyd E. Hawes Collection

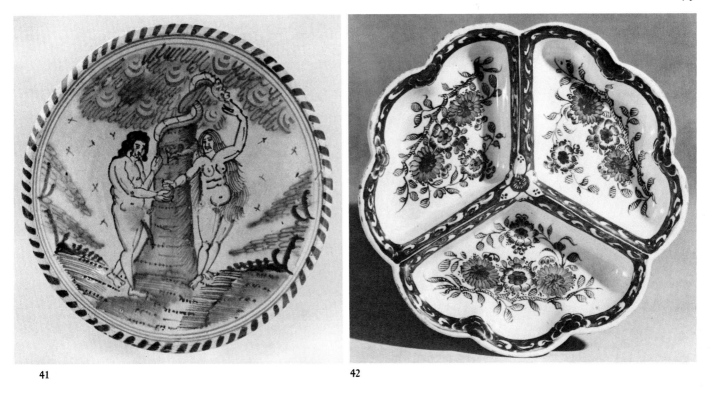

41   42

dishes, bowls, plates, jugs and basins were made. But there were also
tea caddies, teapots, drug jars, tiles, stemmed goblets, posset pots
(covered cups for serving hot thick drinks), vases and other types
of flower containers and pickle dishes (plate 42), as well as saltcellars
and candlesticks, which tended to take the form of those objects rendered in silver. Plenty of wine bottles were made, many inscribed with
the type of wine—such as *Claret*—for which they were intended.
Particularly popular among imbibers were delft puzzle jugs made
with three or more hidden openings; all had to be found and blocked
off before a drink could be enjoyed. There were even delft hand-
warmers, to be filled with hot water and held in a muff; some were in
very fanciful shapes—cats, for example.

English delft was made in large quantities during the seventeenth
and eighteenth centuries. Throughout delft's long history the potters
continued to be inspired by Chinese models. Blue-and-white painting
remained the most common decoration, but in the eighteenth century
there also was polychrome painting, mainly in red, yellow and green,
but in other colors too. Even this palette, some authorities believe, was
derived from Chinese porcelain painted in the *famille verte* style,
so called because of the predominance of green in its decoration.

Very little English delft is marked in any way. Pieces are assigned to
factories on the basis of their style and appearance, and dated inscriptions have been helpful. Although the finest examples are now hard
to come by, delft appears on the market quite frequently. Most auc-
tions of English ceramics feature a delft section.

43.
Unglazed red stoneware coffeepot. English, Staffordshire, c. 1750. Height: 21 cm. (8¼ in.). Unidentified mark. Smithsonian Institution, National Museum of American History, Dr. Hans Syz Collection

Stoneware The first great name in English stoneware, and one of the most historically important in English ceramics, is that of John Dwight (c. 1637–1703), who was making salt-glazed stoneware in Fulham, near London, in the 1670s. Because the imported German Bellarmines were so salable, he concentrated on bottles, but he also produced some extraordinarily fine figurines. Dwight is considered by many authorities to be the first English potter to work in this form.

Among his commercial rivals in Fulham were John and David Elers, who produced unglazed red stoneware that they decorated with applied relief flowers and leaves. The Elerses moved to Staffordshire in the 1690s, where they and their followers became noted for their stoneware tea- and coffeepots (plate 43). Tea and coffee utensils were just beginning to be a popular form of English pottery that would swiftly become indispensable (plates 44, 45 and 46). During the eighteenth century English teapots changed from an early type derived from the Chinese (plate 47) to a later neoclassical form (plate 48). Commemorative items were also made in salt glaze (plate 49).

Stoneware appeared in other parts of England, too. The Morley family made it at Nottingham, and it was manufactured in Derbyshire and Yorkshire. Although production began to slow down after mid-century, the decline was relatively gradual, and salt-glazed stoneware was still being made as late as the 1780s.

44

45

44.
Innumerable teapots were produced in salt-glazed stoneware in England as tea became increasingly popular and prices fell, bringing it into more homes as a daily drink. This globular teapot and cover is decorated with polychrome flowers against a black background pattern of circles and dots; the handle and spout are green. English, c. 1760. Height: 12.6 cm. (4⅞ in.). Unmarked. Smithsonian Institution, National Museum of American History

45.
Creamer shaped like a head of lettuce, with leaf decoration. Salt-glazed stoneware in white. English, Staffordshire, mid-eighteenth century. Overall length: 13.2 cm. (5¼ in.). Unmarked. Cooper-Hewitt Museum, gift of Eleanor Garnier Hewitt

46.
Salt-glazed teapot and cover with crabstock (knotty, gnarled branch) handle, decorated with netlike design painted in yellow, purple, blue and green enamels. English, Staffordshire, c. 1745–70. Height: 9 cm. (3½ in.). Unmarked. Smithsonian Institution, National Museum of American History

46

47

48

47.
Globular salt-glazed stoneware teapot painted overall with purple-red enamel, the white reserve with polychrome flowers. The handle is of the type known as *twig*. English, Staffordshire, c. 1750. Height: 12.7 cm. (5 in.). Unmarked. Smithsonian Institution, National Museum of American History, Joanne Toor Cummings Fund

48.
Stoneware teapot with sliding cover decorated with neoclassical figures and motifs, including anthemia, bellflowers and leaves, in polychrome relief. English, Lane End, Staffordshire, made by John Turner, late eighteenth century. Height: 12.6 cm. (4⅞ in.). Mark: impressed *TURNER*. Cooper-Hewitt Museum, bequest of Erskine Hewitt

49.
Portraits of royalty and commemorations of events connected with it go far back in English pottery. The *G III R* on this salt-glazed brown stoneware jug and the crown and monogram decoration refer to the coronation of King George III in 1760, although the jug was not necessarily made at that time. English, c. 1760–70. Height: 24 cm. (9½ in.). Unmarked. Smithsonian Institution, National Museum of American History

49

Slipware   The traditional lead-glazed slipware turned out in many parts of England in the sixteenth and seventeenth centuries was made of buff or red clay and generally covered with green, black or brown glazes. It was usually decorated with white slip, although sometimes other colors were employed. *Metropolitan slipware* was made around London in the seventeenth century; another important center was Wrotham in Kent. At all these potteries, liquid slip was trailed onto the pieces from a container with a long spout, to form designs consisting of rosettes, sprays, lions or simple dots and dashes. Inscriptions and other commemorative devices to celebrate family or public occasions were also popular.

More elaborate slipware was made a little later in North Staffordshire. In the reign (1660–85) of Charles II, potters there made huge dishes seventeen to twenty-two inches in diameter, which were decorated in slip with royal portraits, heraldic devices or allegorical figures. The most important potter of this ware in the late seventeenth century was Thomas Toft. Slipwares continued to be made well into the nineteenth century.

The Staffordshire Potteries   Toward the end of the seventeenth century the production of slipware and other styles of lead-glazed earthenware began to expand (plates 50 and 51). In the 1760s individual workshops and small potteries began to give way to large-scale factories. Staffordshire was the most important site of this vast growth in pottery making; the area, known simply as the Potteries, has con-

50.
Earthenware cup or mug, decorated with yellow and brown slip. English, c. 1710. Diameter: 12 cm. (4¾ in.). Unmarked. Smithsonian Institution, National Museum of American History, Dr. Lloyd E. Hawes Collection

Colorplate 17.
Two lead-glazed pottery plates with polychrome "tortoise-shell" decoration, made decades apart. The glaze is crackled and has a fine iridescent tone. Left: English, probably from the factory of Thomas Whieldon, Staffordshire, c. 1760. Diameter: 24.3 cm. (9½ in.). Unmarked. Right: English (?), factory unknown, probably nineteenth century. Diameter: 24.4 cm. (9⅝ in.). Unmarked. Cooper-Hewitt Museum, gift of James Fay (plate on left) and gift of the Misses Hewitt (plate on right)

51.
Dishes made in the form of a leaf are a characteristic form of English pottery. Earthenware leaf dish with "twig" handle, probably used for serving. English, c. 1750. Length: 23.2 cm. (9⅛ in.). Unmarked. Smithsonian Institution, National Museum of American History, Dr. Lloyd E. Hawes Collection

tinued to the present day as one of the world's great manufacturing centers for earthenware. Its rise to prominence was due in large measure to geography; Staffordshire had large deposits of many different kinds of clays, plentiful coal to fire the kilns and ample land and water routes to transport materials and finished products.

The earliest of the great eighteenth-century Staffordshire potters was John Astbury (1686–1743). Among his special wares was a red earthenware pottery known as Astbury ware. This was decorated with white clay reliefs under a transparent lead glaze. Astbury's work is closely associated with that of Thomas Whieldon (1719–1795), who was one of the most important figures in the history of Staffordshire potteries.

In his long career at Fenton and elsewhere in Staffordshire, Whieldon made many kinds of pottery: slipware, agate ware (an attractive variegated pottery of different-colored clays), red stoneware, salt-glazed stoneware and creamware. He was constantly experimenting, and he trained many apprentices who later became leading potters and founders of new firms. From 1754 to 1759, Josiah Wedgwood was his partner. Rather unfairly, in view of his great contribution to the new varieties of English ceramics, Whieldon's name is given to just one kind of pottery—Whieldon ware. This is earthenware using different lead glazes to produce a mottled "tortoise-shell" appearance (colorplate 17). Whieldon also made tableware and figurines. The latter includes soldiers, gamekeepers, national heroes (plate 52), mythological figures, equestrians and musicians, in addition to animals (plate 53) and birds (plate 54).

While Josiah Wedgwood was Whieldon's partner, a brilliant green glaze was revived for the first time since the sixteenth century and

52

52.
The patron saint of England, St. George, is shown slaying the dragon in this lead-glazed earthenware group. English, Whieldon type, c. 1750. Height: 28 cm. (11 in.). Unmarked. Smithsonian Institution, National Museum of American History

53.
Water buffalo with "tortoise-shell" glaze, inspired by distant Chinese models. English, probably Thomas Whieldon, c. 1750. Overall length: 24.8 cm. (9¾ in.). Unmarked. Smithsonian Institution, National Museum of American History, Dr. Lloyd E. Hawes Collection

53

used for teapots in the shape of pineapples and cauliflowers. Wedgwood continued to make these popular forms (plate 55) after he left Whieldon; they were also manufactured by other English potters.

The triumph of English ceramics is surely creamware, which was made in Staffordshire—and later in other places—from about the first third of the eighteenth century. Creamware was earthenware the color of heavy cream, lead-glazed, and of a superior, even quality. The ingredients were those used in white salt-glazed stoneware—white clay to which calcined flint had been added—but these were fired at a low temperature instead of the high one needed to produce stoneware. Fired once to produce a *biscuit* (see Glossary), creamware was then glazed and fired again. Thomas Astbury, son of John, is thought to have discovered the process between 1720 and 1740, but it was Josiah Wedgwood (1730–1795) was developed it to its full glory.

From about 1760 on, Wedgwood devoted himself to obtaining a finer quality in the medium. Within five years, after much experimentation, he had produced a creamware that was light in weight, with a good, clear color and a thin, quite brilliant glaze. It was an immediate success. Wedgwood called it "Queen's Ware" (plate 56), after Queen Charlotte, wife of George III, who ordered a creamware tea service in 1765 and gave him permission to use the name.

At first creamware was sometimes decorated in black by transfer printing, a process whereby an illustration from an engraved copper

54.
This unusual pottery dovecote is four-sided, with a pointed top. It is covered with oxide and lead glazes in mottled green and gray. There are forty-two roosting doves. English, Whieldon type, c. 1750. Height: 20.3 cm. (8 in.). Unmarked. Smithsonian Institution, National Museum of American History

55.
Green, yellow and white earthenware teapot in the shape of a cauliflower. English, Wedgwood, c. 1760. Height: 14 cm. (5½ in.). Unmarked. Brooklyn Museum, Winthrop Miles Collection

56.
Queen's Ware (creamware) dessert dish, tray and ladle with overglaze brown decoration. English, Etruria, Josiah Wedgwood, c. 1780. Overall length of tray: 33.7 cm. (13¼ in.). Mark: impressed *WEDGWOOD*. Cooper-Hewitt Museum, bequest of Erskine Hewitt

plate was transferred first to thin paper and then applied to the glaze; a later development was transfer printing in dark red or purple. By 1765 enameling was being used, and a little later, in 1774, Wedgwood made his celebrated 952-piece dinner service, known as the Frog Service, for Russia's Empress Catherine the Great. Decorated in sepia with English scenes, it was also adorned with frog motifs since it was made to be used at the Grenouille Palace near St. Petersburg.

Another of Wedgwood's distinctive developments in ceramics was an unglazed black stoneware that he called "basaltes." This medium, employed mainly for portrait busts and plaques, was also used for vases, urns and pots (plate 57), teaware and services for coffee and chocolate (plate 58). Wedgwood referred to black basaltes decorated with terra-cotta figures in imitation of ancient classical models as "Etruscan ware." He was fascinated by the idea of imitating Etruscan pottery, of which he had a very high opinion because it was then thought that many fine vases (they are actually Greek) had been made by the ancient Etruscans. When he opened a new works at a village about two miles from Burslem in Staffordshire in 1769, he

57.
Black basaltes bulb pot with painted encaustic decoration in terra cotta, white and pink. Modeled black cupids appear against a terra-cotta color ground. After a design by John Flaxman. English, Etruria, Josiah Wedgwood, 1780–1800. Height: 14.5 cm. (5¾ in.). Mark: impressed *WEDGWOOD*. Cooper-Hewitt Museum, bequest of Erskine Hewitt

named the place Etruria; and a red stoneware he produced was christened *Rosso antico*.

One of Wedgwood's greatest discoveries was his jasperware, first sold in 1775. This was a fine stoneware that was colored all the way through by the introduction of metallic oxides. The colors of jasperware were pale and dark blue and green, white, lilac, yellow and black; a few pieces used more than one of these. White reliefs, consisting generally of neoclassical motifs taken from Greek and Roman models, were typical and stood out well against the colored bodies. Jasperware was especially fine for portrait work because it gave the effect of a cameo (plates 59 and 60).

A late Wedgwood innovation, first made in 1779, was pearlware—a very pale creamware with a bluish glaze, an effect achieved by adding a larger proportion of flint to the body than usual. Wedgwood's own firm did not make very much pearlware, but different potteries produced great quantities between about 1790 and 1820. Wedgwood's other innovations, including his basaltes and jasperware, were also copied by his competitors during his lifetime because such wares, being immensely popular, were of course equally profitable.

In addition to his other talents, Wedgwood was an excellent business-man. In 1769 he formed a partnership with Thomas Bentley, a Liver-pool merchant and connoisseur, that was to last until Bentley's death in 1780. Bentley managed the firm's showrooms in London, where the latest products were displayed and sold, often to the nobility. These items are marked *Wedgwood & Bentley* (see colorplate 16). To-

58.
Black basaltes made by Wedgwood has long
been sought by collectors. This set is for
chocolate, a very popular beverage in the
eighteenth century, and consists of a pot
with cover, a sugar bowl with cover and a
creamer. English, Etruria, early nineteenth
century. Overall height of pot: 23.8 cm.
(9⅜ in.). Marks: incised *N* on pot and
creamer and impressed *WEDGWOOD* on
sugar bowl and creamer. Cooper-Hewitt
Museum, bequest of Erskine Hewitt

59

60

day they command premium prices because of their very high quality.

Most Wedgwood is marked, but the study of the marks is not simple. The names *Josiah Wedgwood*, *Wedgwood & Sons*, *Wedgwood & Bentley* and others were impressed at various times. Much eighteenth- and nineteenth-century creamware and other kinds of pottery, though impressed with the mark of *Wedgwood & Co.*, was in fact made by another Wedgwood firm—not the historic one, though also of Staffordshire. Various other enterprises stamped their wares *Wedgewood*, *Wedgwood ware* and even *Vedgwood*, in an attempt to pass for the famous pottery.

During the eighteenth century Staffordshire was full of potters besides the Astburys, Whieldon and Wedgwood. Many of the potteries were so small that it would be impossible to name each one and all its wares. Among the better known, the Wood family of Burslem is notable for producing some of the finest of the Staffordshire figurines that have so long enchanted collectors. Aaron Wood and his brother Ralph were excellent modelers, Aaron working for a time under Thomas Whieldon. He made pew groups showing a man and woman seated together on a high-backed bench in white salt-glazed stoneware (these were also made in earthenware by other potters). Enoch Wood, Aaron's son, did busts of many of the important men of his time, including Voltaire (colorplate 18), John Wesley, William IV and George

59.
Portrait medallions were a Wedgwood specialty and some have American interest. This is William Temple Franklin, illegitimate son of Benjamin Franklin and last royal governor of New Jersey, in white jasper on a blue ground. English, Etruria, Wedgwood, 1785. Height: 10.9 cm. (4¼ in.). Mark: impressed *WEDGWOOD*. Brooklyn Museum, Emily Winthrop Miles Collection

60.
Portrait medallion of Admiral Horatio Nelson in white jasper on dark blue ground. English, Wedgwood, c. 1800. Height: 9.6 cm., 15.2 cm. with frame (3¾ in., 6 in. with frame). Mark: impressed *Wedgwood*. Brooklyn Museum, Emily Winthrop Miles Collection

Colorplate 18.
Portrait bust of Voltaire, glazed and poly-
chromed earthenware. English, probably
Enoch Wood, late eighteenth century.
Height: 20.8 cm. (8⅛ in.). Unmarked.
Cooper-Hewitt Museum, bequest of Erskine
Hewitt

Colorplate 19.
Ceramic portrait bust of George Washington
by Ralph Wood the Younger. English,
Staffordshire, Burslem, c. 1772–95. Height:
25.5 cm. (10 in.). Mark: impressed *Ra Wood
Burslem*. Smithsonian Institution, National
Museum of American History

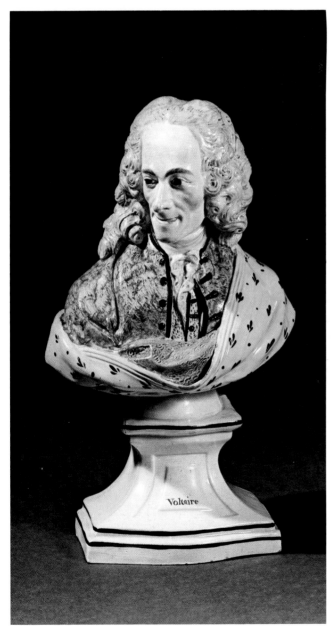

61

Frederick Handel. Ralph Wood and his son (also named Ralph) were makers of Staffordshire portrait busts and figurines (colorplate 19 and plate 61). They are particularly known for their popular Toby jugs: beer mugs in the form of a seated man wearing a tricorn hat.

The potter Josiah Spode worked with Thomas Whieldon. His factory, founded in 1766 at Stoke-on-Trent, produced cream-colored wares and a particularly fine pearlware.

Leeds The Staffordshire potteries of the eighteenth century faced competition from the Leeds Pottery at Hunslet in Yorkshire, which was owned by the Green family and went into production in about 1750. Its outstanding product was again creamware, which was very highly finished and had an unusually smooth, beautifully toned glaze. Some Leeds creamware was decorated in enamels; other pieces were left plain so that the superior glaze could be seen to best advantage. The most admired effect was the pierced openwork decoration, also known as basketwork, which ornamented many pieces (plate 62). A simple hand punch while the clay was still unfired created this effect. The ware was pleasingly light in weight: because a great deal was exported to Europe, having it weigh as little as possible was an advantage.

Leeds produced all the usual tablewares, fruit baskets, potpourri holders, confectionary baskets, trays, teapots and caddies, cruets, inkstands and so on in creamware. Little was marked until the 1790s, after which the name *Leeds Pottery* was sometimes impressed. The marks were irregular, however, and both imitations and forgeries of Leeds ware are known.

61.
Rare equestrian figure of William Augustus, Duke of Cumberland, third son of King George II of England, a general who is most famous for his suppression of the Jacobite forces of Bonnie Prince Charlie at the Battle of Culloden in 1746. The figure, which is lead-glazed earthenware, is glazed in translucent brown, beige, yellow and green, and shows the duke dressed as a Roman soldier. English, Ralph Wood the Elder, c. 1765. Height: 38.1 cm. (15 in.). Unmarked. Smithsonian Institution, National Museum of American History, gift of Ansel Schoeneman

62.
Creamware cup and saucer with pierced openwork design and overall painted decoration in violet and green. English, probably Leeds, c. 1765–90. Diameter of saucer: 14 cm. (5½ in.). Height of cup: 9 cm. (3½ in.). Unmarked. Smithsonian Institution, National Museum of American History, Dr. Lloyd E. Hawes Collection

62

Anglo-American Wares Many British factories made wares specifically for export to the United States. Since the Americans in the eighteenth century did not have a native ceramic industry sufficiently large and well organized to supply their growing needs, they even imported inexpensive English tablewares, which had a good reputation for cleanliness, attractiveness and durability.

Before the American Revolution the wares imported from England by the colonists were merely standard English types. But after the United States was established as a nation, large quantities of earthenware—sometimes known as Anglo-American pottery—were made expressly for American consumers. Several Liverpool factories were very active in supplying this market. They made jugs, plates, bowls and especially pitchers of transfer-printed earthenware. These pieces were decorated with American scenes (colorplate 20), maps, flags and portraits of American heroes, and many had slogans emblazoned on them (plate 63). Typical commemoratives were the memorial jugs issued on the death of George Washington in 1799, inscribed: "Washington in Glory, America in Tears." About three hundred American motifs on Liverpool pottery have been recorded. Very few are marked.

The Staffordshire potteries made more Anglo-American pottery than any other source. They came into their own with the War of 1812, depicting mainly naval engagements and the heroes of both sides, transfer-printed in black-on-white wares. Although these were undoubtedly profitable, it is mildly surprising that British manufacturers should have put out pieces commemorating victories won against their own forces.

63.
Among the wares made for the American market at English potteries was this earthenware pitcher with black transfer-printed decoration proclaiming "Union to the People of America. Civil and Religious Liberty to All Mankind." On the other side is a ship bearing the British flag. English, Liverpool, 1795. Height: 19.1 cm. (7½ in.). Unmarked. Smithsonian Institution, National Museum of American History, Robert H. McCauley Collection

Colorplate 20.
Earthenware pitcher displaying ship's signals at the Portland (Maine) Observatory. The Eastern and Western staffs each have twelve signals and the lighthouse is shown in the center. English, Liverpool, 1810. Height: 23.5 cm. (9¼ in.). Unmarked. Smithsonian Institution, National Museum of American History, Robert H. McCauley Collection

64

65

Colorplate 21.
Arms of the State of Delaware, transfer-printed on a ceramic platter. English, Stoke, Cliff Bank Works (Thomas Mayer), 1829. Length: 42.9 cm. (16¾ in.). Mark: blue transfer-printed eagle holding the legend *E Pluribus Unum*. Smithsonian Institution, National Museum of American History, Ellouise Baker Larsen Collection

64.
Idyllic view of Mount Vernon, transfer-printed in blue with a vessel under sail on the Potomac in the background and a horse and rider in the foreground. English, J. & W. Ridgway, Hanley, Staffordshire, 1814–30. Length: 28.6 cm. (11¼ in.). Mark: *J & W Ridgway*. Brooklyn Museum, gift of Mrs. William C. Esty

65.
Plate showing the Capitol in Washington, D.C., in blue transfer printing. English, Cobridge, Ralph Stevenson, c. 1815–40. Diameter: 25.2 cm. (9⅞ in.) Mark: transfer-printed *R S & R*. Smithsonian Institution, National Museum of American History, Ellouise Baker Larsen Collection

A distinctive form of Anglo-American pottery with transfer-printed monochrome decoration of American subjects made after about 1812 is popularly known as Historical Blue Staffordshire (or Old Blue) because the early wares were decorated in shades ranging from deepest cobalt to a quite pale blue. Later, pink was also used extensively, as well as some sepia, black, green, brown, purple and red, but the dark blue has always been by far the most admired. Inexpensive dinner services, tea services, sets of plates and pitchers were all made in this style for everyday use and sold in the United States in large quantities; it has nonetheless become one of the most popular areas of pottery collecting. This is partly due to nostalgia for the American past, but in addition many of the views used as decoration, executed before the invention of photography, are valued as being among the earliest pictorial representations of certain localities.

About eight hundred subjects on Historical Blue Staffordshire have been identified. A number are simple geographical views of towns and cities (Boston Harbor, Pittsburgh), historical sites (Mount Vernon—plate 64—and the Capitol), outstanding buildings (the Deaf and Dumb Asylum, Hartford) and natural wonders (Niagara Falls). There were depictions of calamities, such as the Great Fire of the City of New York in 1855, and of historical events from the Landing of Columbus (no fewer than fifteen different scenes) to the Opening of the Erie Canal. Another important, highly prized series was known as the Arms of the States (colorplate 21). Many sets of American views were issued, each piece being decorated with a different view and surrounded by a border that varied from maker to maker. Since these borders were very distinctive, they are often a key to the identification of the maker. Firms specializing in American views were Enoch Wood & Sons and J. and J. Jackson of Burslem, and Ralph Stevenson of Cobridge (plate 65). Quite a lot of makers marked their wares, but most of them did so irregularly and working with the marks is not easy.

The Staffordshire potters made other kinds of specialty wares for sale in America. One, called Gaudy Dutch and aimed directly at the Pennsylvania German (misnamed Dutch) market, was an earthenware brightly painted with underglaze blue and overglaze enamel, all in the most vivid shades, including pink, yellow, green and red. The motifs were neither patriotic nor American views, being chiefly floral. Designs are uniformly busy and the general effect is cheerful, almost garish. Gaudy Dutch was primarily tableware that came in patterns, about sixteen of which—with many variations—have been catalogued. Produced from about 1810 to 1830, it was hardly ever marked. Popular with collectors for many decades, Gaudy Dutch is now becoming rare on the market.

After about 1830, British potters made another Anglo-American ware, Gaudy Welsh, so named because it was produced in Swansea, Wales. Heavier and cruder than Gaudy Dutch, it was painted in floral patterns with copper luster or gilding.

Sponged ware (often called "spatter ware")—painted by means of sponges or soft rags dipped into various colors—was made in Staffordshire from about 1820 to 1850 for the American market. Dinner sets, tea sets, water jugs and toilet sets consisting of a washbowl and jug were produced in about forty different patterns. Typical are "Schoolhouse," "Tulip" and "Bird on a Fence." Some of this ware is marked with the name *ADAMS* for the potter William Adams.

Victorian Pottery   The British ceramic industry, the most important in the world, continued to experiment and produce new varieties of earthenware (see colorplate 1) throughout the nineteenth century. Formerly dismissed as merely "Victorian," in recent years these wares have captured a following of students and collectors, and now nearly every variety has its adherents. Technically many of them are of superior quality and, although mass-produced, show considerable distinction. The transfer printing and the painted decoration remain bright after more than a hundred years (colorplate 22).

The array of early nineteenth-century and Victorian wares is amazing. Some forms were continuations of styles developed during the eighteenth century, while others reflected the Victorians' delight in creating their own version of past styles. In Staffordshire, transfer-printed wares (mentioned earlier in the section on Anglo-American wares) were now produced with views of England and foreign

Colorplate 22.
Part of a child's yellow-glazed earthenware tea service decorated with a black transfer-printed design by Adam Buck. English, Newcastle-upon-Tyne, C. T. Maling, mid-nineteenth century. Height of pot: 10.2 cm. (4 in.). Unmarked. Smithsonian Institution, National Museum of American History, gift of Mr. and Mrs. Jack Leon

localities as well—Enoch Wood & Sons alone probably made more than five hundred of these. A wide range of other subjects, including historical, comic, sporting and farming scenes (plate 66), was also rendered in this style. After about midcentury the taste for these transfer-printed wares died away gradually.

Until the 1850s, figurines were made in the round; thereafter, many were flat-backed and consequently less expensive. The glaze was clear, often dazzlingly white, and the figurines were simply and rather sparingly decorated in enamels, especially blue, red, green, yellow and black. Frequently they were inscribed in gold with the name of the subject.

The range of subjects for figures and figure groups is so great that collectors specialize in certain types. Among the most popular were royalty—for example, Queen Victoria and her children—and such military figures as Wellington, Napoleon, Nelson and Garibaldi. Celebrities in every field, even notorious murderers, were portrayed. There were many fictional subjects, often of a sentimental nature: The Lovers, The Fortune Teller, Soldier's Dream, Roman Charity. Theatrical characters were common, including versions of Uncle Tom and Little Eva. Animals, headed by dogs of numerous breeds (plate 67), but including also sheep, horses and bulls, were made in large numbers, as were small models of churches and cottages. Staffordshire figurines

66.
Earthenware side plate decorated with mauve transfer print of a farmer with horses pulling a hay rake. English, Staffordshire, nineteenth century. Diameter, 9.7 cm. (3¾ in.). Unmarked. Cooper-Hewitt Museum, gift of Mrs. Paul Moore

67.
Thousands of pottery dogs, among which the spaniel was high in popularity, were made by the Staffordshire potteries in the nineteenth century. They were originally intended as mantelpiece ornaments. English, Staffordshire, nineteenth century. Height: 24.2 cm. (9½ in.). Unmarked. Smithsonian Institution, National Museum of American History

66

67

SPRING · SVMMER·

·THE·RAINBOW· CELADON & AMELIA

·AVTVMN· ·WINTER·

COMES·JOVIAL·ON ON·SOVNDING·SKATES

68

68.
Tiles were extremely popular in Victorian décor and were used extensively on fireplace surrounds, in conservatories and even on outside walls. Ceramic tiles of the Four Seasons. English, Minton China Works, c. 1880. Width of each tile: 20.3 cm. (8 in.). Mark: impressed *MINTONS*. Smithsonian Institution, National Museum of American History, E. Stanley Wires Collection

69.
The single most famous product of Josiah Wedgwood & Sons for nearly two hundred years has probably been their copies of the Portland Vase. Various editions, differing somewhat from one another, have been made. This is one of the nineteenth-century copies in black and white jasper. English, Josiah Wedgwood & Sons, nineteenth century. Height: 25.5 cm. (10 in.). Unmarked. Smithsonian Institution, National Museum of American History, gift of Paul A. Straub

continued to be made into this century. Very few were marked by the potter, and because they have been so popular, many figurines were constantly reproduced.

Swinton, in Yorkshire, was the site of a pottery that produced a particularly popular nineteenth-century earthenware decorated with a brown lead glaze known as Rockingham glaze, after the Marquis of Rockingham on whose land the pottery was located. This style was later produced in large quantities by other English factories and in North America.

Majolica—an earthenware with brilliant and richly colored glazes —was an immediate success when it was introduced by the Minton firm in Staffordshire in 1850. It was used for tablewares and ornamental items, as well as for such very large pieces as garden seats, umbrella stands and floor vases. Minton produced some of the finest examples of Victorian majolica, and from 1842 on yearly marks were adopted. Many different firms, including Wedgwood, then added this line to their wares while still continuing to create other popular ceramics (plates 68 and 69).

69

70.
The technique of salt-glazed stoneware was revived in late nineteenth-century English pottery factories. This off-white jug, which is incised and decorated in relief, was designed and executed by George Tinworth for Doulton. English, Lambeth, Doulton & Company, c. 1869–72. Height: 25.3 cm. (9⅞ in). Mark: impressed *Doulton Lambeth* in oval with marks of potter. Cooper-Hewitt Museum, gift of L. Bancel La Farge

Colorplate 23.
Three-handled glazed stoneware tankard with incised ornament and a flamingo modeled in relief against a brown stippled ground. Made by Florence E. Barlow. English, Lambeth, Doulton, 1884. Height: 17 cm. (6⅝ in.). Marks: impressed *Doulton Lambeth 1884*; also marks of senior assistants. Cooper-Hewitt Museum, gift of Mrs. Paul Brandwein

Art Pottery   The art-pottery movement, which aimed at the improvement of both design and craftsmanship, was particularly vigorous in England in the latter part of the nineteenth century, where it was part of the larger impetus known as the Arts and Crafts movement. The ceramic wares that emerged as part of this movement are generally referred to as studio pottery.

One of the earliest artist-potters was William de Morgan, who opened a small pottery in Chelsea in 1872. Like many studio potters, he was especially interested in glazes and in lusterware. Indeed, the expressed aim of his pottery was to reproduce the Hispano-Moresque or Renaissance Italian maiolica lusterware. He achieved quick success in making lustered tiles, then went on to work on vases and plaques. The pottery shut down in 1907.

Four brothers of the Martin family were also early studio potters. Working in Southall, Middlesex, they produced Martinware, a distinctive salt-glazed stoneware decorated with incised or relief patterns, which they sold at a shop in London. But their most famous items are extraordinary grotesque birds; some of which have detachable heads. Roughly finished, these pieces are noted for their odd, sometimes fierce expressions, and are believed to have been inspired by Japanese book illustrations. The Martin brothers' pottery closed in 1914; all their ware is marked, but the marks vary.

One of the large established English potteries was also a leader in the nineteenth-century art-pottery movement. The Doulton factory at Lambeth, in South London, revived the production of salt-glaze stoneware (plate 70), and from 1871 permitted students of the Lambeth School of Art to decorate stoneware at its works. Each individual piece was signed by the student. Among the most famous of the student-decorators were the sisters Hannah and Florence Barlow, who specialized in animal and bird motifs (colorplate 23).

The art-pottery movement remained strong in England into this century, and in the 1920s the idea spread that the pot, being such a unique work of art, should be created entirely by one person. This process included, for the first time, such steps as throwing and firing. Some artists even dug their own clay! The most important artist associated with this movement is Bernard Howell Leach (1887–1979), who was born in China of English parents and was strongly influenced by the ceramic art of China and Japan, where he went to teach and stayed to study. Leach's pottery was located at St. Ives in Cornwall. One of his assistants there was Shoji Hamada, who also became a famous potter and later returned to Japan to head a pottery school. Among Leach's other pupils were Katherine Pleydell-Bouverie, noted for the matte glazes she made from plant ashes, and Michael Cardew, who specialized in lead-glazed slipware and later made stoneware in Africa from clays along the Volta River.

9   American Pottery

Colonial America was full of potters—English, Dutch and German—all bringing with them a long and vigorous heritage of pottery making. But for several reasons a sophisticated pottery industry did not emerge until the mid-nineteenth century: the transportation and delivery of both raw materials and finished products were limited and expensive, the population was sparse and demand consequently scant, and it was the policy of the British government to restrict all colonial industries. Those who wanted, and could afford, luxurious decorative ceramics were well supplied by imports, primarily English delft, Staffordshire earthenware and German salt-glazed stoneware. It was not until the second quarter of the nineteenth century, after the new nation was firmly established, that American potters began to create decorative wares of a quality to rival the products of British and European factories. Later these wares would become more and more distinctively American in form and decoration, and ultimately a number of distinguished artist-potters emerged who, drawing on the European and the Oriental heritages, produced works recognized all over the world as outstanding contributions to ceramic art.

Although very few pieces of colonial American pottery are signed, hundreds of potters and their works have been identified. Actual records of potters working in New England and various parts of the South go back to the middle of the seventeenth century. A utilitarian red earthenware known as redware was by far the most common type during this period.

Redware was made from common brick clay, which was plentiful all along the Eastern Seaboard, and fuel for the potters' kilns was abundant in almost every district. Small local potteries made quantities of household pots, bowls and mugs, generally turned on a wheel and fired in small kilns at relatively low temperatures. Many of these

Colorplate 24.
A small "library" of flint-glazed bottles made in imitation of books. American, Bennington, Vermont, Lyman, Fenton & Company, c. 1849–58. Heights, from left to right: 20.7 cm. (8⅛ in.), 15.6 cm. (6⅛ in.), 26.7 cm. (10½ in.). Unmarked. Smithsonian Institution, National Museum of American History, gift of Mrs. Harold G. Duckworth

wares were covered with a clear lead glaze; the finished products were reddish-brown, often attractively streaked or mottled because of impurities in the clay and irregularities in kiln temperatures (plate 71). Others were dark brown or black, when manganese was present in the glaze, or occasionally green, the result of copper oxide. Surface decoration, consisting of simple patterns, wavy lines and sometimes inscriptions, was either "scratched" onto the surface using the sgrafitto technique or trailed onto the ware with a white or cream-colored slip. An important center for the manufacture of such redware by the mid-eighteenth century was Walachia, North Carolina, where the United Brethren (Moravians) made high-quality pottery that they sometimes sold at public sales.

The earliest recorded attempts to make a stronger ware, fired at a higher temperature, took place in Burlington, New Jersey, in the 1680s under the auspices of one Daniel Cox. In 1689 he wrote:

> I have erected a pottery att Burlington for white and chiney ware, a greate quantity to ye value of 1200 li have been already made and vended in ye County, neighbour Colonies and ye Islands of Barbados and Jamaica where they are in great request. I have two houses and kills with all necessary implements, diverse workmen, and other servants. . . .

In spite of his enthusiasm, Cox's attempts to emulate porcelain, or even delftware, failed soon thereafter.

71.
Large red earthenware punchbowl covered with a clear lead glaze with brown streaks. American, 1769. Diameter: 31.7 cm. (12⅓ in.). Incised on front *I F 1769*. Unmarked. Smithsonian Institution, National Museum of American History

Colorplate 25.
Stoneware pitcher with blue incised bird and
foliage decoration. American, Philadelphia,
probably by John Remmey III, c. 1815.
Height: 22.3 cm. (8¾ in.). Mark: *JR*.
Brooklyn Museum

Colorplate 26.
Red earthenware pie plate by David Spinner, incised on front: *Go for half a Joe* and *David Spinner Potter*. American, Pennsylvania, c. 1800. Diameter: 29.2 cm. (11½ in.). Unmarked. Brooklyn Museum, gift of Mrs. Hulda Cail Lorimer

72.
Sgraffito-decorated Pennsylvania German plate by Johannes Neesz, inscribed with a quotation in German that reads in translation: "I have been riding over hill and dale and everywhere have found drink." The galloping horseman, shown here holding a gun, is characteristic of this ware. American, Tylersport, Montgomery County, Pennsylvania, 1800–1825. Diameter: 31.8 cm. (12½ in.). Unmarked. Smithsonian Institution, National Museum of American History

In contrast, the manufacture of salt-glazed stoneware was highly successful. By the latter part of the eighteenth century stoneware had generally replaced simple redware for certain types of utilitarian objects. Unlike redware, stoneware requires a rough clay, often bluish in color, that can tolerate intense heat. The best source for such clay in the colonies was around Staten Island, New York, and South Amboy, New Jersey, and much early American stoneware was made fairly close to this vein. William Crolius, a New York potter, is believed to have set up the earliest important high-temperature stoneware kiln in America in 1730, and members of the Crolius family continued to work in the medium for over one hundred years. Another family dynasty of stoneware potters started with John Remmey, who opened a factory in New York in 1735. Several generations of Remmeys carried on the business in New York, South Amboy and Philadelphia (colorplate 25). As American transportation improved and clays could be shipped greater distances, stoneware began to spread to other areas, particularly New England.

Stoneware was used for all sorts of utilitarian objects and was generally gray or a bluish gray, decorated in cobalt blue. Some designs were scratched, some trailed, some drawn freehand. The decoration of these early wares, which accounts for much of their charm in the eyes of collectors, consisted of abstract floral and geometric patterns.

The Revolution rudely interrupted the flow of superior European wares into the colonies and gave incentive to American potters to replace imports with comparable domestic wares. Although some redwares continued to be made during the early years of the nineteenth century, they were now much more richly decorated and ornamental, and experiments with kiln temperatures and glazes—often with the help of experienced immigrant English potters—led to more ornamental stonewares and new types of earthenware. After 1850 factories, with a desire to increase production, designed products to be made from molds in order to bring out large quantities.

During the early period of the Pennsylvania German settlements, a distinctive form of decorative redware that was essentially a colorful and charming peasant ware was popular. Some decorations were done by trailing slip, others by the sgraffito method. Motifs typically incorporated tulips and other flowers, double-headed eagles (the symbol of the Habsburgs), the Tree of Life and humorous inscriptions. The range of articles was very wide: it included cake molds, flat filled with water and blown. Large plates intended solely for display were also made in the sgraffito technique by such artists as David filled with water and blown. Large plates intended solely for display were also made in the sgraffito technique by such artists as David Spinner (colorplate 26), Georg Hübner and Johannes Neesz (plate 72). These Pennsylvania German redwares reflected a strong German influence, as did much of the material culture of the Pennsylvania Germans.

73.
Hound-handled pitcher in Rockingham glazed earthenware with a scene of a stag being brought to bay on the body. American, East Liverpool, Ohio, Harker, Taylor & Co., c. 1850. Height: 28 cm. (11 in.). Mark: *Harker, Ta.* impressed in circle. Smithsonian Institution, National Museum of American History

Decorative redware was produced in quantity in the Shenandoah Valley below Pennsylvania throughout the nineteenth century and well into the twentieth. Among the best-known potters were Peter Bell and his sons John, Samuel and Solomon. Their works included jugs with lion-head and dolphin handles, mirrors adorned with patriotic eagles, as well as delightful grinning lions with yellow-glazed bodies and curly brown manes made by John and Samuel for their nieces.

In the post-Revolutionary period stoneware was used increasingly for certain kitchen wares because it was stronger and more impervious than redware. Typically, the pottery produced by Captain John Norton, who opened a factory in Bennington, Vermont, in 1793, was described as "good honest" stoneware. However, stoneware grew increasingly ornate throughout the nineteenth century, and in addition to scratched and drawn designs, molded relief became popular. Representational motifs largely replaced the earlier abstract decorations. Birds and flowers were particularly evident, but other subjects—lions, flags and clipper ships—are found. Some figurines, mainly of dogs and lions, were made in this medium. Sometimes names are die-stamped onto a piece, but they are not always those of the potter; they may be those of the wholesaler.

As more and more large kilns were built to create high-fired stoneware, experiments revealed that the same common clay used to produce low-fired redware could produce a stronger, paler pottery if

74.
Rockingham ware creamer in the shape of a standing cow, the tail forming the handle and the mouth the spout; there is also a triangular opening in the center of the back that was used to pour the cream into the container. Brown, flint-glazed earthenware. American, probably Jersey City, New Jersey, mid-nineteenth century. Length: 17.2 cm. (6¾ in.). Unmarked. Cooper-Hewitt Museum, gift of the Misses Hewitt

fired at a hotter temperature. The result was yellow ware, used largely for serviceable items; but a further development was Rockingham ware—one of the most important American ceramics of the nineteenth century. (The name of the ware was apparently derived from its resemblance to the form of English brown-glazed earthenware made in South Yorkshire, although no direct link has been established.) It was created by adding a brown glaze to the fired clay, usually giving the finished product a mottled appearance. Various methods of spattering or sponging the glaze onto the ware account for the extremely wide variations in color and add to the interest of collecting Rockingham. An advanced form of Rockingham was flint enamel, created by dusting metallic powders onto the Rockingham glaze to produce brilliant varicolored streaks.

Articles for nearly every household activity and ornament could be bought in Rockingham ware: dishes and bowls, of course; also bedpans, foot-warmers, cuspidors, lamp bases, doorknobs, molds, picture frames, even curtain tiebacks. All these items are highly collectible today and all are eagerly sought. A few Rockingham specialties command particular affection among collectors and correspondingly high prices. The best known of these, perhaps, is the celebrated hound-handled pitcher (plate 73), made in many sizes. A second famous Rockingham design was the "Rebekah at the Well" teapot, showing the Old Testament figure of Rebekah in relief beside the well with her jar. And a third form of Rockingham that endeared itself to the public was the creamer in the shape of a cow, produced from about 1840 (plate 74). Rockingham poodles (plates 75 and 76) have been popular, as have the numerous flasks made in the shape of books (see colorplate 24). Though the United States Pottery Company of Bennington, Vermont, is the best known of the makers of Rockingham glazed pieces, many factories from New Jersey to Ohio produced these wares.

In the last quarter of the nineteenth century American potters turned out the earthenware with a colorful lead glaze called majolica. Characteristically it was decorated in relief with flowers, leaves, birds and fish, all realistically depicted and painted in green, brown, pink, blue, lavender and other colors. The usual forms were made for use at table in patterns such as "Strawberry," "Water Lily" and "Daisy"; but majolica was also used for tiles, vases, figurines, jugs with tree-branch handles and pitchers in the form of open-mouthed fish. Quite a bit of American majolica was marked. Today many pieces are on the market, where collecting by pattern is particularly popular.

All these many kinds of nineteenth-century wares were produced at a number of factories in the East and the Midwest, and molds were designed by many talented individuals. From the point of view of the collector, the firms described below are perhaps of greatest interest.

The D. & J. Henderson pottery, established in Jersey City in 1828, was the earliest major factory of the period. It became the American Pottery Manufacturing Company in 1833, the American Pottery

Company in 1840, and the Jersey City Pottery Company from 1845 until it closed in 1854. Famous for its emulation of Staffordshire pottery—including transfer-printed wares—this pottery earned for Jersey City the label "Staffordshire of America." Under the guidance of one of the original founders, David Henderson, the factory introduced the use of molds, which other potteries quickly copied. Molded stoneware, yellow ware and Rockingham were produced in quantity and were all of superior quality. While working at the Henderson factory, the famous English modeler Daniel Greatbach designed the popular hound-handled pitcher mentioned earlier.

Another series of well-known potteries operated in Bennington, Vermont, between 1844 and 1858. The first was established by Julius Norton (grandson of the stoneware potter Captain John Norton) in partnership with his brother-in-law Christopher Webber Fenton. Christopher was a brilliant artist who launched Bennington on the road to producing decorative and ornamental wares. Known first as Norton & Fenton, the partnership produced yellow ware, molded stoneware, scroddled ware (a form of agate) and such a variety of Rockingham-style pieces that true Rockingham products are often erroneously called Bennington ware. The mistake may have originated because the potters in Bennington marked their Rockingham lines more regularly than did potters in other parts of the country; indeed, since most other Rockingham is not marked at all, the erroneous conclusion was that it was all made in Bennington. The Norton-Fenton partnership

75 and 76.
A pair of poodles in Rockingham glazed earthenware. American, Bennington, Vermont, 1849–58. Heights: 21.3 cm. (8⅜ in.) and 21 cm. (8¼ in.). Unmarked. Brooklyn Museum, H. Randolph Lever Fund

77.
Two views of a barrel-shaped stoneware cooler decorated in blue. One shows the ever-popular standing and reclining deer, while the other depicts the equally well-loved lion and bird. American, Bennington, Vermont, c. 1850–51. Height: 61 cm. (24 in.). Mark: *J & E Norton* stamped on front. Smithsonian Institution, National Museum of American History, Lura Woodside Watkins Collection

lasted from 1844 to 1847. In 1848, Fenton acquired two new partners, Lyman and Park; but by the following year, 1849, the firm had become Lyman, Fenton & Company. At this time Daniel Greatbach was associated with the enterprise and flint enamel was invented there by Fenton. The final stage in this sequence lasted from 1853 to 1858, when the Fenton firm was known as the United States Pottery Company. Meanwhile, until 1894, various members of the Norton family continued to produce decorative earthenwares and stonewares (plate 77).

To the south, English-born Edwin Bennett opened another important pottery in Baltimore in 1846, which he operated for some years with his brother under the name E. & W. Bennett. It was here that a Rockingham "Rebekah at the Well" teapot was produced, and later the firm was particularly noted for its majolica ware. As westward expansion took place in the 1840s, East Liverpool, Ohio, became a major pottery center for stoneware, yellow ware (plate 78) and Rockingham, made from clays found along the Ohio River.

Successful though the American mass-produced ceramics were in the latter part of the nineteenth century, there were those who regretted the inevitable artistic compromises. As in Continental Europe and England, there was a reaction from American artist-potters who often set up studios and workshops where they could revive the techniques used by individual craftsmen and create one-of-a-kind pieces.

One of the earliest American art potteries was the shop usually known as the Chelsea Keramic Art Works, although the firm's name changed many times. At Chelsea, Massachusetts, Alexander W. Robertson had begun a pottery in 1866, making flowerpots and other humble wares; but at the instigation of his brother, Hugh, and father, James, who joined him in turn, an ambitious art-pottery opera-

78.
Yellow ware pitcher with molded relief decoration, including rams' heads inside four arches. American, East Liverpool, Ohio, C. C. Thompson Pottery Company, late nineteenth century. Height: 23.8 cm. (9⅜ in.). Unmarked. Smithsonian Institution, National Museum of American History

Colorplate 27.
Vase and plate by the Rookwood Pottery. American, Cincinnati, Ohio. Vase height: 21.4 cm. (8⅓ in.). Mark: impressed Rookwood Pottery mark; also label of Louisiana Purchase International Exposition, St. Louis, 1904. Plate diameter: 31.2 cm. (12¼ in.). Mark: impressed *Rookwood 1885*; plate dates to early twentieth century. Cooper-Hewitt Museum, gift of J. Lionberger Daviss (vase) and anonymous gift (plate)

79.
The Dedham Pottery Company made a type of pottery they called "volcanic ware," typified by this vase decorated with running thick green glaze over a light gray glaze. American, Dedham, Massachusetts, late nineteenth or early twentieth century. Height: 19.7 cm. (7¾ in.). Mark: *Dedham Pottery HR*, incised. Smithsonian Institution, National Museum of American History, Dr. Lloyd E. Hawes Collection

80.
Stoneware canteen with an olive-colored glaze, showing a hunting scene. American, attributed to Dedham Pottery Company, Chelsea, Massachusetts, late nineteenth century. Height: 22.3 cm. (8¾ in.). Mark: *HR*. Smithsonian Institution, National Museum of American History, gift of Mrs. Marcus Benjamin

80

tion was launched in 1872. At first the firm produced copies of Greek vases. Later Hugh, a persistent experimenter, developed a stoneware that was glazed in an oxblood color after the model of the much-admired Chinese *sang de boeuf*, and another ware with a unique crackled glaze, also inspired by Oriental models. In 1896, the Robertson firm moved to Dedham, Massachusetts, and was renamed the Dedham Pottery Company. Very fine pieces were produced by this family, each one individually decorated in freehand (plates 79 and 80).

Perhaps the leading American art pottery was Rookwood, founded in Cincinnati in 1880 by Maria Longworth Nichols (later Mrs. Bellamy Storer). Its origin was the direct outcome of the popularity of ceramic painting as a pastime for ladies. At that time an active group in Cincinnati known as the Women's Pottery Club invited Maria Nichols, who came from a wealthy family of art patrons and was an accomplished ceramic artist, to join the group. However, some confusion arose about her invitation, and despite the fact that the group kept one place open for eleven years, she never became a member. Instead, she set to work independently in a studio above the wagon shed of the Dallas Pottery in Cincinnati. After a short period her father gave her a schoolhouse, where she set up her own works. She named the new pottery Rookwood, after the family home where she had grown up.

At the Rookwood Pottery the clay was turned on a potter's wheel, each piece thus being unique. Vases were the most usual form, and like so many of the European potteries toward the end of the nineteenth century, Rookwood was greatly influenced by Japanese design with its emphasis on exquisite glazes (colorplate 27). Mrs. Storer's enthusiasm for Japanese wares was so strong that she engaged a Japanese designer, Kataro Shirayamadani, who had come to America as a member of a Japanese village that toured the United States. He was to become Rookwood's most famous artist and was particularly noted for the fineness of his underglaze painting. The Rookwood glazes were predominantly shades of yellow, brown, green, red and white, and had an extraordinary glossiness. Particularly admired was a shimmering crystalline glaze known as Tiger Eye.

Each Rookwood piece was signed by the designer. Before 1886, many marks were employed. After that, the initials *RP* (with the *R* reversed) were used, and for each year from 1887 to 1900 a flame was added over the initials. After 1900, Roman numerals were added to represent dates. In a further complication, certain letters indicating the shape of the vase and its clay color are found on some pieces, and the artists signed in various ways, though usually with their initials. Rookwood went into bankruptcy in 1941, but its wares have since been much studied and catalogued.

Other art potteries flourished during this period in many parts of the United States. In Zanesville, Ohio, Samuel A. Weller began to produce wares similar to Rookwood but on a much larger scale in 1895, and also introduced a distinctive iridescent ware that combined different metallic lusters (plate 81). The Newcomb College Pottery, associated with Tulane University in New Orleans, first put its art pottery on the market in 1897. The clay was thrown by experienced potters, but the decorations were done by students who emulated a variety of styles, ranging from Oriental to folk designs, and also produced works in the Art Nouveau manner beginning around 1900. In Boston, the Grueby Faïence Company, founded in 1897, was noted for its

81.
Plaque of metallic lusterware, a specialty of the Weller Pottery Works; this one was decorated by Jacques Sicard. Such classically inspired portrait plaques, representing the Victorian image of beauty, were popular in the latter part of the nineteenth century. American, Zanesville, Ohio, 1896. Dimensions: 43.3 x 33 cm. (16¾ x 13 in.). Mark: signed *Weller Sicard*. Smithsonian Institution, National Museum of American History

82.
Ceramic vase with a bright green matte glaze on the exterior and a glossy pinkish-gray glaze on the inside. American, Colorado Springs, Van Briggle Pottery Company, 1902. Height: 26.7 cm. (10½ in.). Marks: incised Van Briggle symbol and name, *1902* and *III*. Smithsonian Institution, National Museum of American History, gift of the Van Briggle Pottery Company

leaf-shaped wares with matte green glazes. Here the forms were designed by George P. Kendrick and the glazes developed by William H. Grueby.

Around the turn of the century Louis Comfort Tiffany opened a ceramic works in Corona, New York, and added pottery to his Art Nouveau creations. In Colorado Springs, Artus Van Briggle, a former decorator at Rookwood and perhaps America's leading Art Nouveau potter, created his celebrated vases adorned with fluid, elongated birds and plants (plate 82). When he died in 1904, at the time of the Louisiana Purchase International Exposition in St. Louis—where his pottery won several prizes—the showcases of his work were draped in black in his honor. In sharp contrast, George E. Ohr, the maverick potter of Biloxi, created over six thousand brilliantly executed but eccentric pieces. Often twisted, dented and folded, they ranged in subject matter from his version of a Rough Rider's hat to a vase as tall as a man.

In the twentieth century American studio potters have been noted for their work with new glazes, especially on stoneware. Among the most important potters working in this medium have been Gertrud and Otto Natzler in California (plate 83) and Fong Chow in New York (plate 84). In recent years, the art of ceramics has been widely taught in American art schools and colleges and is undergoing an enormous renaissance among studio potters. Today, America is an acknowledged leader in the revival of pottery as a true expression of individual artistic creativity. The craft has entered the mainstream of art and has developed along parallel lines, supplying examples in styles ranging from Abstract Expressionism to Minimalism and Pop. Yet the basic vessel—first shaped so many aeons ago—remains fundamental to the potter's art.

83.
Stoneware vase by Gertrud and Otto Natzler, glazed in earth tones of brown and gray. American, 1946. Height: 11.5 cm. (4½ in.). Unmarked. Cooper-Hewitt Museum, gift of Edward J. Wormley, in memory of Gertrud Natzler

84.
Pomegranate-shaped vase in mottled black and brown glazed stoneware by the Chinese-American potter Fong Chow. American, Alfred, New York, 1956. Height: 10.5 cm. (4⅛ in.). Marks: signed with Chinese character and incised *Chow*. Cooper-Hewitt Museum, anonymous gift, in memory of Monica Loretta Smith

10   Advice for
Pottery Collectors

Since pottery appeared so early as a product of civilization and has been produced in quantity by virtually every culture, the number of pieces available to the collector is overwhelming. Most collectors have thus tended to specialize, some collecting pottery from a specific country or region, others collecting related forms. It is also common to collect a particular style or technique, or the work of a particular artist, studio or factory.

Pottery offers the same pleasures and perils to the would-be collector as any other comprehensive area of antiques, and requires the same meticulous study to ensure that a collection develops and expands in quality, not just quantity. Highly competitive and expensive areas of pottery collecting (sixteenth-century Italian maiolica, for instance) may be an appealing but unrealistic first step in building a collection; but even within such an area there are possibilities for acquiring secondary pieces. Other, more available fields—twentieth-century industrial pottery, for example—are very feasible. Thus, a collector of pottery has a wider range for acquisition than in many other fields of antiques. It also should be stressed that beginning collectors have an equally wide margin of potential error in selecting the finest from such a bewildering choice, and questions of authenticity, quality and condition must always be considered when buying.

Pottery is an important part of most museum collections, and pieces are frequently available for study at shops, galleries and auction houses. When on information-gathering expeditions to other collections, it is often useful to carry a small notebook and make brief notes or even thumbnail sketches of particular forms, decorations, glazes, condition details and marks. Often, translating a visual impression into such a written record, however brief, fixes important characteristics of the piece in one's mind, and encourages visual acuity and perception. It is

Colorplate 28.
Red earthenware coffeepot by Thomas Haig & Company. American, Philadelphia, c. 1825. Height: 27.3 cm. (10¾ in.). Metropolitan Museum of Art, New York, Rogers Fund, 1922

particularly valuable to begin such note-taking with pieces that are documented, signed, dated or otherwise described or authenticated (museums are the finest resource for such study). These "primary" objects will provide a foundation for later individual judgments as to the age, provenance and quality of the hundreds of pieces an ambitious collector will undoubtedly encounter.

Whenever possible, handle as much pottery as you can. Through direct experience of the material one gains expertise in the correct weight and texture of the various pottery bodies and glazes. Be sure to look at all aspects of a piece: note carefully the overall form, color and appearance and also how the glaze is applied, how the interior is finished and how the underside appears in relation to its age or origin.

Each foray into the museum or marketplace should be buttressed by as much reading as possible. Most areas of pottery history, many public and private collections and a number of important individual works have been researched and published. A reading list is essential to familiarize yourself with the existing literature on the subject. Some of the books may be expensive; before choosing a specific title it is always a good idea to consult your library, where it may be available for reference or loan. There are a good many books on pottery marks; however, bear in mind that not all marks have been recorded and published, and your new acquisition may require some intense (but pleasurable) detective work.

Plenty of professional and amateur organizations exist to promote the study and appreciation of ceramics. Such groups as the American Ceramic Circle provide a forum for experts, collectors and students to share their knowledge and queries. Seminars and courses on pottery are offered through museums. If you write to an expert for information on a piece, be sure to include a clear description of it, drawings of any marks that appear and, whenever possible, a good photograph.

The precautions urged on collectors in other areas of antiques also apply to collectors of pottery. Buy only from reputable dealers who are willing to provide a written statement regarding the age and origin of a piece. Examine every object carefully for its condition, noting any repairs or alterations (many repairs are deceptively expert). Always keep "quality" uppermost in your mind when considering the enduring value of a piece of pottery.

Finally, do not assume that a collection of pottery must include only antique pieces. Many talented living potters offer their works at reasonable prices through studios, galleries or at periodic exhibitions and fairs. Today's superb pieces will be the antiques of tomorrow. A purchase of high-quality contemporary work will not only provide pleasure for the owner but also stimulate enthusiasm among artists and other collectors for this time-tested and traditionally respected art.

Glossary

agate ware, a variegated earthenware made of different colored clays. It was frequently used by Thomas Whieldon in Staffordshire in the eighteenth century.

basaltes ware, an unglazed black stoneware perfected by Josiah Wedgwood in Staffordshire in the eighteenth century.

biscuit, pottery that has been fired once but not glazed.

black figure, a technique used by ancient Greek potters whereby figures were drawn in black on a reddish clay ground.

body, the mixture of clay and other ingredients out of which pottery is made. (Also called "paste.")

celadon, the European (originally French) name given to Chinese stoneware glazed in a color, derived from iron oxide, that varies from delicate green to gray-blue.

chinoiseries, fanciful European interpretations of motifs, patterns and compositions believed to be characteristic of Chinese ornament. At times during the seventeenth and eighteenth centuries, chinoiserie was fashionable in all the decorative arts.

crackle, a glaze that has been crazed accidentally or on purpose to produce a system of cracks. Highly developed in China, crackle decoration has been used extensively by nineteenth- and twentieth-century Western potters.

crazing, the formation of a mesh of fine cracks over the surface of a glaze.

creamware, a superb lead-glazed earthenware the color of heavy cream. A creamware developed by Josiah Wedgwood in Staffordshire in the eighteenth century was known as Queen's Ware.

Delftware, tin-glazed earthenware produced in the Netherlands and taking its name from the town of Delft, where it was made on a large scale in the seventeenth and eighteenth centuries.

delftware, tin-glazed pottery made in England, sometimes resembling that produced in the Netherlands.

earthenware, a type of pottery made of common clays, such as red clay. Though hard and brittle, it is slightly porous.

enamels, a finely ground vitreous substance, often containing brilliant color, used for overglaze painting of pottery. Enamels fuse onto the surface of the fired glaze at relatively low temperatures.

faience, the term used by the French for tin-glazed earthenware from the sixteenth century onward. It is derived from Faenza,

a major Italian center for this type of ware in the fifteenth century.

flambé glaze, a glaze derived from copper which turns a rich red mottled with blue when fired in reducing kiln atmosphere.

glaze, a glassy coating, based on a combination of silica and a fluxing agent such as lead oxide, applied to pottery. Glazes may be clear, transparent, highly colored or opaque.

Hausmaler, an independent (freelance) decorator who painted pottery in his home or outside the factory.

high-temperature colors, a range of colors used in underglaze painting that can withstand the high temperature required to fix a glaze. Green, purple and yellow are possible, but blue and red are the most common.

incised motifs, designs cut into unbaked clay, or through a layer of slip or glaze, with a sharp instrument.

istoriato wares, pottery decorated with scenes from stories, primarily biblical and mythological. They were particularly characteristic of Italian maiolica of the sixteenth century.

jasperware, a fine stoneware that may be colored all the way through its body by the introduction of metallic oxides. Colors range from pale blue to green, lilac, yellow, maroon and black.

kiln, a special oven used to fire clay to varying degrees of hardness.

lead glaze, a coating of silica and lead oxide that becomes glassy when applied to hardened clay and fired; lead glaze may be colored green or brown by adding copper to the mixture.

luster, an iridescent metallic film on pottery produced by painting the surface of an already glazed and fired pot with a metallic oxide and firing it again at a lower temperature.

luting, using slip to attach pieces of unfired pottery together, such as relief decoration, handles and other elements.

maiolica, the generic term for tin-glazed earthenware made in Italy, derived from Majorca, from where much tin-glazed pottery was exported to Italy.

majolica, nineteenth-century earthenware with rich colored glazes, popular in both England and America in the Victorian era.

overglaze painting, decoration applied to pottery after it has been glazed and fired. Enamels were frequently used for this type

of decoration, particularly those whose colors were compatible with the lower temperatures of the secondary firing necessary to fix them to the surface.

pearlware, a creamware with a bluish glaze developed by Josiah Wedgwood in Staffordshire in the eighteenth century.

porcelain, a hard, white, translucent ceramic made by firing pure clay and glazing it with variously colored fusible materials.

porcellaneous, ceramic bodies that have some of the attributes of porcelain. The term is usually applied to certain types of highly vitrified stoneware.

red-figure painting, a technique used by ancient Greek potters whereby a black ground was laid on a red clay, silhouetting figures left in the color of the ground.

redware, a generally utilitarian form of American pottery made of common brick clay.

reserve, a section on pottery kept free of background color and reserved for decoration.

salt glaze, a glaze, used on stoneware, produced by throwing ordinary salt into the kiln during firing. The reaction of the clay and the vaporized salt results in a slightly pebbled surface.

sang de boeuf, a copper-red glaze, Chinese in origin, copied by potters everywhere.

scroddled ware, the term for nineteenth-century American pottery made of striated clays of different colors; similar to English agate ware.

sgraffito, decoration incised on a pot after it has been dipped in slip or glaze.

slip, a mixture of fine clay and water used in the manufacture and decoration of pottery; also used in luting pieces of pottery together.

slipware, pottery on which slip has been used for decoration.

sponged ware, or spatter ware, pottery decorated by applying colors with sponges or soft rags. Many pieces were made in Staffordshire in the nineteenth century for the American market.

sprigging, molded decoration applied as relief ornament to pottery.

stoneware, a type of glazed or unglazed pottery that is fired to a high temperature, above 1200 degrees Celsius, making it impermeable to liquids.

three-color glazes (San-ts'ai), a form of decoration, frequently seen on pottery of the T'ang dynasty, consisting of shades of yellow, green and blue.

throwing, making a pot (or another circular object, such as a deep dish) by pressing clay while it is on a rotating wheel.

tin glaze, an opaque white glaze resulting from the addition of tin oxide to a siliceous lead glaze. Maiolica, faience and delft are all tin-glazed wares.

tortoise shell, an earthenware with a mottled appearance created by the use of differently colored lead glazes. It is sometimes called Whieldon ware after Thomas Whieldon of Staffordshire, who perfected it in the eighteenth century.

trailing, the process of making a design on earthenware by dripping liquid slip onto a piece of pottery.

transfer-printed decoration, a process whereby a design from a specially inked copper engraving is transferred to the surface of glazed pottery through the use of a thin paper transfer.

underglaze painting, painting applied to glaze a piece of pottery prior to firing. The decoration thus fires at the same high temperature as the glaze, and a limited range of colors, known as high-temperature colors, can withstand the heat.

vitrification, the process in which certain clay bodies, under great heat, undergo chemical changes that make them extremely hard, and impervious to liquids, even without a glaze.

yellow ware, a nineteenth-century American pottery created by firing the common clay that is used to make redware at a higher temperature, thus producing a stronger, paler ware.

Reading and Reference

General

BIRKS, TONY. *The Art of the Modern Potter.* New York: Van Nostrand Reinhold, 1976.

CHAFFERS, WILLIAM. *Marks and Monograms on European and Oriental Pottery and Porcelain.* 2 vols. 15th rev. ed. London: W. Reeves, 1965.

CHARLESTON, ROBERT J., ED. *World Ceramics.* New York: McGraw-Hill, 1968.

COX, WARREN E. *The Book of Pottery and Porcelain.* 2 vols. New York: Crown Publishers, 1944.

CUSHION, J. P. *Handbook of Pottery and Porcelain Marks.* 4th ed., rev. and exp. London and Boston: Faber and Faber, 1980.

HETTES, KAREL, AND P. RADA. *Modern Ceramics: Pottery and Porcelain of the World.* London, 1965.

HONEY, WILLIAM B. *The Art of the Potter.* London: Faber and Faber, 1946.

——. *European Ceramic Art from the End of the Middle Ages to about 1815.* 2d ed. London: Faber and Faber, 1963.

The Ancient World

CHARLESTON, ROBERT J. *Roman Pottery.* London: Faber and Faber, 1955.

LANE, ARTHUR. *Greek Pottery.* London: Faber and Faber, 1948.

The Far East and the Lands of Islam

GRAY, BASIL. *Early Chinese Pottery and Porcelain.* London: Faber and Faber, 1953.

HONEY, WILLIAM B. *The Ceramic Art of China and Other Countries of the Far East.* London: Faber and Faber and the Hyperion Press, Ltd., 1945.

JENYNS, SOAME. *Japanese Pottery.* New York: Praeger Publishers, 1971.

LANE, ARTHUR. *Early Islamic Pottery: Mesopotamia, Egypt and Persia.* London: Faber and Faber, 1947.

——. *Later Islamic Pottery: Persia, Syria, Egypt and Turkey.* London: Faber and Faber, 1957.

MEDLEY, MARGARET. *The Chinese Potter: A Practical History of Chinese Ceramics.* Oxford: Phaidon, 1976.

MILLER, RAY A. *Japanese Ceramics.* Rutland, Vt.: C. E. Tuttle Co., 1960.

Europe

BEMROSE, GEOFFREY. *Nineteenth Century English Pottery and Porcelain.* London: Faber and Faber, 1952.

DUCRET, SIEGFRIED. *German Porcelain and Faience.* Translated by Diana Imber. New York: Universe Books, 1962.

FROTHINGHAM, ALICE WILSON. *Lustreware of Spain.* New York: Hispanic Society of America, 1951.

GARNER, FREDERICK H. *English Delftware.* London: Faber and Faber, 1948.

GIACOMOTTI, J. *French Faiences.* Translated by Diana Imber. New York: Universe Books, 1963.

GODDEN, GEOFFREY A. *British Pottery and Porcelain, 1780–1850.* London: A. Barker, 1963.

HONEY, WILLIAM B. *English Pottery and Porcelain.* Revised by R. J. Charleston. London: A. & C. Black, 1962.

——. *Wedgwood Ware.* New York: D. Van Nostrand Co., 1949.

KORF, DINGEMAN. *Dutch Tiles.* Translated by Marieke Clarke. London: Merlin Press, 1963.

LANE, ARTHUR. *French Faience.* New York: Praeger Publishers, 1970.

LIVERANI, GIUSEPPE. *Five Centuries of Italian Majolica.* New York: McGraw-Hill, 1960.

RACKHAM, BERNARD. *Italian Maiolica.* London: Faber and Faber, 1963.

——. *Early Staffordshire Pottery.* London: Faber and Faber, 1951.

REILLY, R., AND D. SAVAGE. *The Dictionary of Wedgwood.* Woodbridge, Suffolk: Antique Collectors Club, 1980.

ROSE, MURIEL. *Artist-Potters in England.* London: Faber and Faber, 1955.

TOWNER, DONALD C. *English Cream-Coloured Earthenware.* London: Faber and Faber, 1957.

WAKEFIELD, HUGH. *Victorian Pottery.* London: H. Jenkins, 1962.

United States

ALEXANDER, DONALD E. *Roseville Pottery for Collectors.* Richmond, Ind.: Privately published, 1970.

ARNEST, BARBARA M., ED. *Van Briggle Pottery.* Colorado Springs: Fine Arts Center, 1975.

BARBER, EDWIN A. *The Pottery and Porcelain of the United States: An Historical Review of America's Ceramic Art from the Earliest Times to the Present Day.* New York: G. P. Putnam's Sons, 1909.

BARNES, BENJAMIN H. *The Moravian Pottery: Memories of Forty-Six Years.* Doylestown, Pa.: Bucks County Historical Society, 1970.

BARRET, RICHARD C. *Bennington Pottery and Porcelain: A Guide to Identification.* New York: Crown Publishers, 1958.

CLARK, GARTH, AND MARGIE HUGHTO. *A Century of Ceramics in the United States, 1878–1978.* New York: E. P. Dutton, 1979.

HAWES, LLOYD E. *The Dedham Pottery and the Earlier Robertson's Chelsea Potteries.* Dedham, Mass.: Dedham Historical Society, 1968.

KIRCHER, EDWIN J., BARBARA AGRANOFF AND JOSEPH AGRANOFF. *Rookwood: Its Golden Era of Art Pottery, 1880–1929.* Cincinnati, 1969.

PECK, HERBERT. *The Book of Rookwood Pottery.* New York: Crown Publishers, 1968.

Some Public Collections
of Pottery

Index

Numbers in *italics* indicate pages on which black-and-white illustrations appear. Numbers in **boldface** indicate pages on which colorplates appear.

Acknowledgments

Cooper-Hewitt staff members have been responsible for the following contributions to the series: concept, Lisa Taylor; administration, Christian Rohlfing, David McFadden and Kurt Struver; coordination, Peter Scherer. In addition, valuable help has been provided by S. Dillon Ripley, Joseph Bonsignore, Susan Hamilton and Robert W. Mason of the Smithsonian Institution, as well as by the late Warren Lynch, Gloria Norris and Edward E. Fitzgerald of Book-of-the-Month Club, Inc.

The Cooper-Hewitt Museum wishes to thank the following for their kind assistance: Armin Allen; Susan H. Myers, Jennifer Oka and J. Jefferson Miller II of the National Museum of American History; and Ann Adelman and Neal T. Jones.

Credits

Courtesy of The Brooklyn Museum: plates 55, 59, 60, 64, 75, 76; color 16, 25, 26. Cooper-Hewitt Museum: *endpapers*, figure 1; plates 1, 3, 17, 20, 21, 22, 23, 24, 25, 26, 27, 28, 30, 32, 33, 35, 36, 38, 39, 40, 45, 48, 56, 57, 58, 66, 70, 74, 83, 84; color 1, 7, 9, 10, 12, 13, 17, 18, 23, 27; all photographs by Helga Photo Studio, Inc., except plates 1, 17, 36, 40, 48 and 70 by Cooper-Hewitt Museum, New York. The Hispanic Society of America, New York: 16. The Metropolitan Museum of Art, New York: plates 2, 5, 6, 7, 8, 9, 11, 12, 13, 18, 19; color *frontispiece*, 2, 8, 11, 14, 15, 28. Courtesy of Oxford University Press: figure 2. Smithsonian Institution (Freer Gallery of Art): plates 4, 10, 14, 15; color 3, 4, 5, 6. Smithsonian Institution (National Museum of American History): plates 29, 31, 34, 37, 41, 42, 43, 44, 46, 47, 49, 50, 51, 52, 53, 54, 61, 62, 63, 65, 67, 68, 69, 71, 72, 73, 77, 78, 79, 80, 81, 82; color 19, 20, 21, 22, 24; plates 31, 46, 49, 51, 54, 62, 65, 67 and 78 by Helga Photo Studio, Inc.

Caftleford-Pottery